W9-CMP-107

THE BOOK
OF LIGHT

THE BOOK OF LIGHT

Ask and Heaven Will Answer

ALEXANDRA SOLNADO

ATRIA PAPERBACK

New York London Toronto Sydney

ATRIA PAPERBACK

Atria Paperback
A Division of Simon & Schuster, Inc.
1230 Avenue of the Americas
New York, NY 10020

Copyright © 2007, 2008, 2009, 2010 by Alexandra Solnado
English-language translation copyright © 2010 by Alexandra Solnado

Originally published in Portugal in 2007 by Editora Pergaminho SA.

Translated by Lorvit Borrego

All rights reserved, including the right to reproduce this book or portions thereof in any form whatsoever. For information address Atria Books Subsidiary Rights Department, 1230 Avenue of the Americas, New York, NY 10020.

First Atria Paperback edition April 2011

ATRIA PAPERBACK and colophon are trademarks of Simon & Schuster, Inc.

For information about special discounts for bulk purchases, please contact Simon & Schuster Special Sales at 1-866-506-1949 or business@simonandschuster.com

The Simon & Schuster Speakers Bureau can bring authors to your live event. For more information or to book an event, contact the Simon & Schuster Speakers Bureau at 1-866-248-3049 or visit our website at www.simonspeakers.com.

Designed by Akasha Archer

Manufactured in the United States of America

10   9   8   7   6   5   4   3   2   1

Library of Congress Cataloging-in-Publication Data

Solnado, Alexandra.
   The book of light : ask and heaven will answer / Alexandra Solnado; [translated by Lorvit Borrego].—1st Atria paperback ed.
      p.   cm.
   1. Divination. 2. Spirit writings. 3. Jesus Christ (Spirit) I. Title.
   BF1755.S6613 2011
   248.2—dc22

                                                      2010041157

ISBN: 978-1-4516-1157-1
ISBN: 978-1-4516-1162-5 (ebook)

When you think you already know the answers,
life comes along and changes the questions.

AUTHOR UNKNOWN

This is the book that provides you with new answers
to your latest questions.

JESUS

TABLE OF CONTENTS

INTRODUCTION

You are the reason I created this book.

How many times have you had doubts? How many times have you spoken to me without ever really believing that I would answer you? How often have you tried to contact me and not succeeded?

This book is for you. For you who are reading these words at this very moment. It is my attempt to communicate with you, to help you deal with your anxieties.

These are texts of light that will fill you with energy. I hope they will help to enlighten you on the fundamental issues you face on a daily basis.

I wish to close the distance between us.

For each question, you must choose two symbols (included in this book). These symbols are characters from the alphabet of Aramaic, the language I spoke when I was down there on earth, two thousand years ago.

At the point where the two symbols meet (see table of symbols) you will find a message from me concerning the question you asked. These are my comments on the situation.

This is not just any book. It is a book on communicating with heaven. When you choose your two symbols, you need to understand and believe that everything has a purpose, and that I, up in heaven, will be able to use my messages to teach you great things.

Talk to me, and I will answer you through these texts. This symbolic language I send you is a way of making you rethink your intentions, but, more important, it is a way for you to feel my energy. Read the texts slowly and carefully, and open your heart so that I may enter, so that you may "feel" rather than "think" the answer.

Before choosing the symbols, focus on me. Try to calm your spirit; breathe deeply three times. Then concentrate on me. Open your heart and receive my energy.

Next, focus on an issue that is worrying you. Do not ask questions. Do not ask anything, just think about the issue and how you would like to see it addressed. I will approach it from heaven's point of view. Up here, we have spiritual wisdom, as well as a bird's-eye view of your existence.

I will comment on the issue. There will be times when I may admonish you, other times in which I praise you.

Don't be too concerned about these reprimands. I am not angry at you. I simply want to help you find your way.

As for the praise you receive from me, make the most of it, but don't let it go to your head. Be wary of your ego.

You may be on the right path, but if you become too complacent, the ego will be lying in wait to take control.

Arrogance is the ego's greatest method of attack. Your ego convinces you that you are better than others, better than your brothers. Not only is this not spiritual, it stops evolution in its tracks.

When I reprimand you, try to listen to me without feeling guilty. Guilt does not exist. When you make a mistake, there is always tomorrow to set things right. What matters most is that you choose according to who you are and not in accordance with what others expect of you.

When I praise you, you may feel happy, you may feel extremely happy, but do not lose your center. Be humble. You are all equal. No one is better than anyone else. Different, maybe, but never better.

Do not ask the same question more than once on the same day. Wait for the following day. Time has always been a good mentor, and tomorrow you may find that the subject carries a different energy.

If for some reason you ask the same question more than once (on different days) and the information you receive appears to contradict itself, it means that the issue you are concentrating on is complex and dual. It is an issue that contains polar opposites and therefore needs twice as much attention.

Last but not least, do not forget that you can always count on me when in doubt. Talk to me, ask me questions. If you have continued to ask me questions without ever really believing that you would receive a clear and unequivocal answer, now you have these texts of light that I have prepared for you.

Never again will your questions go unanswered. I will be here to address the issues in your life, at any hour of the day or night. I had hoped to become closer to you, to guide you, and fortunately, we have succeeded. Now all we have to do is begin.

I am ready to start coming into your life. I hope you will receive my teachings as well as you have received me.

JESUS

HOW TO OBTAIN ANSWERS
FROM *THE BOOK OF LIGHT*

To ask a question:

- Find a comfortable place in which to sit.
- If possible, put on some soothing music and light some incense.
- Visualize a white light invading your body.
- Visualize a white light invading the symbols.
- Focus on a person or situation.
- *The Book of Light* will analyze the energy of those concerned and then comment on the situation.
- In this book, Jesus answers all of the questions put to him. His answers are not objective. He only comments so that each of you may then go on to find your own answer. Remember that no one in heaven infringes upon our free will. They may guide and enlighten us, but when it comes down to it, we are the ones who make the final choices concerning each issue.
- Never ask the same question twice in one day. If you want to know more, try again the following day.
- Pick out the symbols slowly, always focusing on the situation or person.
- Go to the table of symbols. The first symbol you pick out belongs to the vertical column. The second symbol belongs to the horizontal column.
- At the point where the two symbols meet, you will find a number that is related to your question.
- Read each message three times so that you take in the meaning, and see how it fits your question.
- If a message appears more than once (regardless of the question asked), it is because it applies to your life in general, to your being, to you as a person.

HOW TO CREATE COINS

If your edition of the book does not come with coins, there are a couple of options for making them yourself:

1. Visit www.alexandrasolnado.net, where you'll find the symbols. Print and cut them out.
2. Be creative and draw your own symbols. Refer to the back of the book to see what they should look like. You can also cut the images out of that page.

SELECTING THE SYMBOLS

Selecting the symbols is a ritual.

It is a movement outside the boundaries of time.

It takes but a thousandth of a second between choosing the symbol and taking it.

This is how long I need to put things in order, to transfer vibrations, to replace the signs so that everything happens as it is meant to happen.

Before picking out the symbols, focus on your heart and really concentrate on the subject you want to address.

The deeper you concentrate, the more at one you will be with the Universe and, as a result, the greater your communication with these messages.

The act of removing the symbols is the question in itself. The answer lies in the conjunction of these symbols.

Scientists say that the conjunction of symbols is always random.

I say that it is always magical.

The force of the earth lies in the selection of these pieces. It is an act of free will that shows man's enormous desire to move ahead.

These symbols will appear exactly as they need to appear.

So that I may answer you.

To put a question to my book, *The Book of Light,* is to accept the message you receive. It may not always be what you wish to hear.

And since I do not lie, the answers you will receive may be bitter or sweet, depending on the truth being spoken.

I will always love those who are willing to hear the truth.

JESUS

TABLE OF SYMBOLS

Once you have picked the first symbol, find where it lies on the vertical line. Next, pick out the second symbol and find where it lies on the horizontal line. At the point where the two symbols meet, you will find the number of the message that is heaven's inspirational answer to your question.

SECOND SYMBOL

FIRST SYMBOL

	𐤀	𐤁	𐤄	𐤇	𐤈	𐤌	𐤊	𐤎	𐤂	𐤒	𐤆	𐤑	𐤋	𐤏	𐤔	𐤕	𐤐
𐤀		1	2	3	4	5	6	7	8	9	91	92	93	94	183	184	185
𐤁	10		11	12	13	14	15	16	17	18	95	96	97	98	186	187	188
𐤄	19	20		21	22	23	24	25	26	27	99	100	101	102	189	190	191
𐤇	28	29	30		31	32	33	34	35	36	103	104	105	106	192	193	194
𐤈	37	38	39	40		41	42	43	44	45	107	108	109	110	195	196	197
𐤌	46	47	48	49	50		51	52	53	54	111	112	113	114	198	199	200
𐤊	55	56	57	58	59	60		61	62	63	115	116	117	118	201	202	203
𐤎	64	65	66	67	68	69	70		71	72	119	120	121	122	204	205	206
𐤂	73	74	75	76	77	78	79	80		81	123	124	125	126	207	208	209
𐤒	82	83	84	85	86	87	88	89	90		127	128	129	130	210	211	212
𐤆	131	132	133	134	135	136	137	138	139	140		141	142	143	213	214	215
𐤑	144	145	146	147	148	149	150	151	152	153	154		155	156	216	217	218
𐤋	157	158	159	160	161	162	163	164	165	166	167	168		169	219	220	221
𐤏	170	171	172	173	174	175	176	177	178	179	180	181	182		222	223	224
𐤔	225	226	227	228	229	230	231	232	233	234	235	236	237	238		239	240
𐤕	241	242	243	244	245	246	247	248	249	250	251	252	253	254	255		256
𐤐	257	258	259	260	261	262	263	264	265	266	267	268	269	270	271	272	

This is my book, *The Book of Light*.
In light lies universal wisdom,
the archetypes of profound experiences on earth.
I will send you profound yet simple inspirations,
which are both real and mystical.
My communication will vary. Each of you who takes
out the symbols in search of an answer will obtain
the message you need at that specific time.
Heaven's movement is perfect. It does not
send people more than they can handle.
Only those who have the power to change their lives do so.
How does it work?
It is simple, as is everything that comes from heaven.
You pick out two symbols.
You will receive an answer from light
based on the number you obtained.
The Book of Light is my book. It is my voice.
It is the answer that I have longed to give you.

JESUS

THE BOOK
OF LIGHT

MESSAGES

1
The Beginning

Divine action begins with light.

It begins with a higher light.

A light that belongs up in heaven.

A heaven that is represented by a channel.

Whenever this channel is open, it means that things are still under control and that there is still the possibility for light to triumph over darkness.

This is how things work.

The energies have to be in their rightful place in order to achieve the harmonization of opposites.

Whenever the forces of *yin* dominate our being, it means that ascension may take place and that this is a spiritual matter.

Ascension is what all human beings strive for, and one-half of their lives will always necessitate spiritual care.

When *yang* prevails, it means that density is rising again and you should do your best not to lose your internal guidance.

This is a temporary explanation. We will renew contact again shortly.

JESUS

2
Floating

This matter has already been brought up before the council of gods; it has been presented at the meetings of the beings of light.

This matter has been dealt with and approved by the higher energy.

Man approves.

Heaven approves.

Man has complied with heaven's will. Everything is in communion.

But in order to move forward with this contract, we need to gain inspiration from the creator. Each and every connection is welcomed and even necessary if this project is to be concluded. Up until now, we have listened to heaven and followed the energies' wishes, yet the project has not been completed. More information is required, more inspiration is needed. I mean, from up here, of course.

Look for the signs. Do not force things. Try to work out which way the currents flows.

Float. For now, it is important to stay afloat, to respect the waves' frequency, to understand heaven's meaning.

When you have finally understood everything, you may proceed, but only when you have reached this point.

Everyone will be pleased with the outcome.

You will open up the way, down there.

And we, up here, will bless your actions.

JESUS

3
Loss

Everything that happens in the Universe is for a reason. The energetic movements of the cosmos are perfect and offer advancement through loss and gain, attachment and detachment. The things that you procure in life are sent to you whenever you conquer something in heaven.

But the things you procure are meant to be used and enjoyed. People should not become attached to them.

If you become attached to something or someone, you will not understand why you have to lose them, when the time arrives.

You thought that this thing or person belonged to you. You thought that it was forever.

If you understand that everything in life is on loan to you, when the time comes to lose what you have conquered, you will remain calm because you know that something else will turn up to help you continue on your evolution.

If you believe that that person or thing belongs to you, when the hour of departure arrives, you will see yourself as a victim, criticize those you believe are taking from you, and end up feeling angry.

Anger is a failure to accept the natural order of things.

Take a closer look at things. Try to understand why you attracted that loss. If you are unable to understand and end up getting angry, each and every action that you take will be tainted by the energy that comes from this anger.

Consequently, it will not be in harmony with heaven.

Things will not be resolved.

Try to understand what it is that motivates you to move forward, anger or acceptance.

A being who accepts is a being who is protected by heaven.

JESUS

4

Inaction

All of heaven has spoken. It has stated what it wants, and it has shown why it has come.

All connections are complete, the links have been made.

A lot of preparation went into making sure that this matter could move ahead. And it can, for it mirrors the will of light.

Human beings, however, continue to be inactive. They do not move forward. They are scared or ashamed or believe that information is still missing. They continue to wait for signs. All the signs have been given. It is time to act.

Just as it is up here, there is a right time for everything down there, a time in which to thrive. If man does not act, this time will pass, and everything will lose its luster, its original timing.

Do not let this time pass you by, do not be afraid. Do not remain at a standstill. Go. Move forward. Do what you know needs to be done. That is all.

Heaven will help with the rest.

There is a time for waiting and a time for action. Now is the time for action.

Do not let it pass you by.

JESUS

5

Deliverance

Man waits patiently for instructions from heaven. He trusts completely in heaven. He has learned which path to follow, and he has learned how to keep his path protected.

The man who delivers himself over to heaven makes life easier for himself. He stops experiencing loss, he stops having to fight for everything. His life is a river where water warmly flows.

He is committed to his mission, and he succeeds in this mission. The path ahead no longer holds secrets, because fear no longer exists. There is only faith and deliverance.

Successive reincarnations have taught man how to stop struggling, how to flow.

When things are going well, he moves ahead.

When something is wrong, he delivers it up to heaven.

This deliverance is your light, your shining light. Everything is in its place.

Man flows, heaven commands, and the two continue the journey in harmony.

JESUS

6

Purpose

When you were up here, before reincarnating, you were given a mission.

All souls go to earth with a mission. To have a purpose in life is part of the experience.

Survival in itself is not a spiritual purpose.

Working only to make and accumulate wealth is not a spiritual purpose.

Experience, for example, is a purpose. To go through certain experiences in order to discover your confines and the extent to which your spirit can participate, this is a purpose.

However, once people are born they tend to focus only on their own survival.

The most important spiritual values are annulled in the name of survival. In the name of survival, we disregard our true reason for being.

Nothing happens unless you have a purpose in life. And even then, nothing spiritually worthwhile will ever happen if you focus only on material return.

Look inside yourself and question the purpose of each initiative. What purpose does it serve? How does this help humanity or the people closest to you?

Why are you doing this? Is it for you, so that you feel more complete, or is it so that you have some material or emotional return?

Look into your heart and feel.

And you will find the answer.

JESUS

7

Harmony

Earth is on earth, heaven is in heaven. There is a favorable time for everything, and there is always an appropriate way of doing things.

Man receives, heaven gives.

Man understands what he needs to do, and only then does he act. He has no ego, he has no guilt, and he has no fear.

His trust in heaven is liberating. Faith helps him to understand the unpredictable; acceptance smoothes the rough edges.

I enjoy seeing how everything comes into harmony once things are in their rightful place.

Success. Luck. Inspiration.

Heaven manifests itself through signs. You are aware of this and are able to read these signs. Everything fits together. Everything is justifiable.

We wish you luck.

This is the path, continue on it.

You will be blessed.

JESUS

8
Flowing

You are in harmony with heaven and all of heaven is in harmony with you.

We talk, and you are able to hear us. When one is willing to do this, it can yield only positive and long-lasting benefits.

Just like a flowing river that does not wish to map out its course, but goes where destiny takes it.

This is your truth. You go where you are taken, and you are happy this way. This is a sublime attitude, and heaven thanks you for it. It will all work out well.

Whatever it is, it will be what is best for you.

JESUS

9
Distance

Distant is that time when things once flowed. Once upon a time, there was a happy person who had made many life-plans. At that time Professor Agostinho da Silva used to say, "Do not make plans for life so as not to ruin the plans that life has made for you."*

That is the feeling. That is the consensus.

Happiness existed long ago but is now so far away. Do not blame others. Do not blame heaven. Do not blame us.

You are entirely responsible for the sadness you feel. There is no guilt, but there is accountability. You have created a distance between heaven and earth.

You do not hear us talking to you, and so you believe that your actions are justified.

We speak through the rain that falls, through the sun that shines. And also through the obstacles that we place before you, so that you may notice us.

Shorten the distance that exists between us. Look up.

Acknowledge us, and we will be eternally grateful.

Nothing makes sense if heaven and earth are not in communion.

JESUS

---

* Agostinho da Silva (1906–1994) was a Portuguese philosopher, essayist, and writer. And that is the feeling. That is the consensus.

10

Conviction

One of the most powerful weapons a spiritual being possesses is his conviction in the journey he is taking. When a being knows where he is at, why things happen, and how to learn from them, his journey becomes both luminous and resplendent.

The conviction that this is the right path attracts untold energy. And when this path is traveled with the dexterity of a king, it, too, becomes more convinced of its victory.

Meditation is always the key.

Conviction is the answer.

Even if there are times when the road does not appear harmonious, you should use the chaos to reconnect and come to heaven to obtain information.

Life will then become prosperous and abundant.

JESUS

11

Compensation

Compensation is a reaction to deep-rooted fear. You are scared, so you try to make up for this feeling.

Why do you not face your fear? Why do you not let yourself feel your fear?

To experience an emotion means to allow that emotion to disappear.

Whenever your fear of experiencing an emotion forces you to opt for something else, it is obvious that this will not help you.

Whenever you choose to do something because it will bring you comfort and rid you of the latent discomfort you are feeling, it is obvious that this action will not be in harmony with heaven.

If you feel bad, stay with this feeling. Let yourself feel your pain, cry as much as you need to.

Rest assured that light will eventually follow.

On reaching deep into your inner self, you will receive enlightenment, in all senses.

After reaching your innermost depths, you will feel much better. However, if you still wish to do something, if the urge persists, go ahead and do it.

JESUS

12

Taking Charge

There are times in our life when we have to take charge.

Not on every occasion. But when it is time, there is no escaping it.

Taking charge is about action. But it is not just action. It means to act and to provoke others into taking action. It is about organizing armies, creating strategies . . . and moving forward.

There is no space here for the heart, or for great sentimentalism. You just do what needs to be done.

This is one of matter's many facets. Not everything is exact, not everything is definitive. Heaven usually asks for connection, feeling, heart, and intuition.

It rarely asks you to put together armies and to attack just because the time is right. Time has run out.

Now . . . it is time.

JESUS

13
Guilt

Guilt is ego.

And who are you? What on earth makes you believe that you are indispensable? What makes you think that the world cannot revolve without you, that life cannot move ahead without you?

Guilt is a person's unconscious attempt to gain power and become indispensable.

Those who feel guilty are usually somewhere doing something, yet believe they should be somewhere else, doing something completely different. This is why they feel guilty. They live in permanent conflict. They do not relax or let others relax.

The guilty person suffers yet has an enormous tendency to blame others.

He thinks, "If I cannot do what I like doing, neither should so-and-so. If I have to be on guard against one thing or another, and if I have to do things I don't like to do, then others should have to do the same."

Why do you demand so much from yourself?

Why do you demand so much from others?

Guilt prevents you from living; it prevents you from looking at yourself.

It is one thing to blame yourself for something you did, another to blame yourself for something that you should have done, and quite another to blame yourself for not fulfilling other people's needs.

Think about this, it may help you:

When person X or Y is suffering, he is meeting his needs; he consciously or subconsciously chose this situation so that through this lesson—through his search to find solutions to his problems—he can evolve.

Consciously, he wants or needs you to look after him, but only up to a certain point. There comes a time when your extreme concern becomes prejudicial to him. And you have your own evolution to go through. If you blame yourself eternally for what you have failed to do, you cannot take care of your own evolution.

It is important to connect, to meditate. From up here, you will be able to distance yourself and see life differently. You will come to understand that every form of dependency is a prison. Those who are dependent are imprisoned. Those who feel guilt are imprisoned. Come up to heaven to feel the lightness of freedom.

JESUS

14
Energy

To ascend means to rise up to heaven. To rise up to heaven in spirit while your body remains on earth. Is it possible to do this during your existence, while you are still alive?

Yes, of course it is. When your consciousness fully expands and travels the path to heaven, it opens up the channel for energy to descend. Energy then descends and invades the whole of one's physical body. It changes frequencies and cleanses misery.

It begins to vibrate.

With heaven's energy, man is able to change all of his paradigms down there on earth. He changes lifestyle. He begins to emit a new frequency.

This frequency is called essence.

This frequency attracts abundance.

This being has ascended.

JESUS

15

Feeling

Man is extremely close to a breaking point. Everything is falling apart; things seem to be on the verge of ruin.

Stretching your emotions to the limit is one of the most powerful feelings that exists.

It is what hurts the most. It is what makes you feel that you are approaching the end.

Feel, let yourself feel completely, every last drop of blood, every last drop of sweat.

And after facing this torment—after having endured the thrashing of these emotional waters, after the subsiding of your pain—you will be left with a feeling of peacefulness that is liberating.

A being lives his emotions to the limit.

He suffers and cries, not because he feels attracted to pain but because he knows that he will not be rid of this pain until he has let himself feel it.

A being goes through all the emotions he is meant to experience, and only once he has overcome his grief does he raise his head to begin a new journey.

This is the reason for loss. It is there to make you stop.

To stop, in order to feel . . .

To stop, so that you can go through all your emotions and advance on your journey, once you have learned the lesson.

Whenever you reach a crossroads in your life, the lessons you have learned will provide you with yet another opportunity to make choices in accordance with who you truly are.

JESUS

16

Dream

You are being impractical.

Any experience proposes harmony between two opposites. And you are leaning toward only one of these two sides.

You dream, and we up in heaven love dreams.

You wish for things, and we up in heaven defend those who have hopes and desires.

You have not yet realized that you need to reconcile heaven and earth.

All dreams require a solid foundation.

Sometimes dreaming is a form of escape. The more you dream, the more you run away from reality.

And you are only dreaming.

We here in heaven are not against dreaming. But you cannot only dream; there comes a point when you have to try to make this dream come true.

Always remember that a dream made into a reality is evolution. A dream that is simply dreamt and followed by more dreaming is a means of escape.

Which do you choose?

JESUS

17

Money

Money is energy. And people use their energy as they see fit. They spend it. Spend it wisely or poorly, on themselves or on others. This energy is yours, and here it is your free will that reigns, telling you what to do. I think we understand each other so far.

However, when it comes to getting back this energy, to regaining this energy, things get a little more complicated.

You want and need money, right? I understand, but try to follow my line of thought.

Why do you buy things, why do you spend money on certain items?

Is it because you feel like spending money?

I believe that the answer is no.

Do you feel like writing a check and handing the money over so that the person you are interacting with can have a better lifestyle?

No, I don't think so.

Could it be because this person wants a new car and needs to earn your money to purchase it? Is that why you buy certain items?

Once again, the answer is no.

So let's see. You don't buy things just because you feel like spending money, nor because you wish that that person had a better lifestyle, and even less so because you want to help him purchase a new car.

No, I believe that these are definitely not the reasons.

You wish to buy something because that item will contribute to improving your life in one way or the other, right?

Am I right?

Okay. Think about this.

You don't use your money as a way of making someone else's life better, but as a way of improving your own.

However, when you think about making money, you completely invert this system.

If I ask you today, to tell me honestly, why you want to or need to make money, you will naturally answer:

"I need to make money because I want to have money, because I want to improve my life and eventually have a new car.

"The money I make does not meet my needs; therefore I need to earn more."

And this is the energy that you send out into the Universe.

To sum up: you would never spend money on helping others better their lives, but you would like someone to spend money on you so that you can improve yours. You would never spend money so as to help someone buy a new car, but you would like someone to spend money on helping you buy a new car.

Do you see how you are wishing that others would do what you yourself would never do?

Do you realize that this will never work?

Nonetheless, you are willing to spend your money on something that would help make your own life better. This is what your money is spent on. Others do the same.

But instead of focusing on making money, focus on this:

"How can I help people improve their lives in different ways?"

When you begin to work on something (a product, an idea, a job, etc.) because you know it would help to improve your life, this is when you will start to make money.

Don't forget. Money is energy you exchange. By itself, it is worth nothing.

If you simply desire it, it runs away. If you have something good to exchange for it, it will come to you.

Stop thinking about money, and focus on how you can contribute to improving people's lives (in whatever way possible), and not only will you receive money, but you will feel fulfilled and be proud of what you do.

And maybe then you will find that you don't really need a new car after all.

JESUS

18

Emotion

Emotion is the starting motor of life. An experience that does not involve emotion is not an experience. It is simply matter in motion. And matter in motion is of no significance. Even the wind makes matter move. It does not require human intervention.

We need human beings to give feeling to experiences, to give soul to things.

And the feeling that people give to things or events sets free an energy that has no limits. Emotion makes the world go round; it makes people move within the world.

Emotion makes children grow and projects prosper. It reduces distances and makes life happen.

Which issues deserve our attention? Those that rouse our emotions. When you do not put your soul into things, you are like a stone waiting for time to pass, waiting to die, so that one day you may have the chance to be reborn with a different conscience, with a different purpose, with a different emotion.

Does the subject you have in hand right now stir up your emotions? What kind of emotion? Which part of you are you putting into things?

Meditate. Close your eyes, breathe, and ask yourself this:

"Which part of myself am I putting into this experience, my mind or my heart? Do I have everything worked out to the very last detail, or does everything begin only with a deep desire?" If you chose the second answer, move forward.

JESUS

19

Opening Up

Begin to open up, especially your heart. Each new situation in life requires you to open up just a bit more.

To open up to new opportunities, and stop being wrapped up in your expectations.

The world has much more to offer than you can ever imagine. But you need to open up your mind and, more important, your heart.

Open up so that you may learn, receive more, and avoid becoming stagnant by doing only what you already know and what is familiar to you.

Open up. Open everything up. Open yourself up to the world.

Open up your mind and your capabilities. Do not get stuck in the same old routine.

First and foremost, open your heart. Your heart is your privilege. Your heart will allow you to detect flaws, deceptions, or successful opportunities.

It will be your heart that intuitively discerns what is and what is not right for you.

And only once you have understood which path to take on this journey may you move forward.

Your moon will then light up the fields you pass through, and the fields themselves will nurture you in your moments of hesitation.

Open up to heaven. Open up to earth, and learn that everything, absolutely everything, in the Universe is committed to infinity.

JESUS

20
Health

Your health should come first and foremost. And this doesn't mean just your physical health. Your spiritual health is also important.

Despite your need to get on with things, to knock down barriers, to overcome obstacles, and to push yourself beyond your limits, it is important that you first consider this:

"If I have a weak body that may fall sick at any moment (think about this even if you are in perfect health), if I have a body with limitations, it is a sign that I must respect my body and know when it is time to stop."

Knowing when it is the right time to take action is hard enough, but knowing when to stop is even harder.

When the body can no longer hold out, when the spirit whispers that it is unable to move forward, stop being stubborn and stop insisting on things that you cannot physically or spiritually achieve.

Stop. Look inward. Go deep into yourself.

Remain there. Just simply remain where you are.

Let go of impulses and illusions.

Remain alone with yourself.

Remain there until you hear life calling you once again toward a series of battles, which no doubt will run more smoothly now that you have refined your weapons.

JESUS

21
Experience

You have to do what you have to do. You have to go through the things you need to go through.

Everything that appears before you in life is to be lived and experienced to the fullest.

If you try to run away from things, you will only end up delaying this thorny journey that you are required to pass through.

Whenever you attract an event, person, or situation in your life, whenever this confrontation takes place, it is because it is time for you to experience this at the deepest level you are capable of.

If you neither wanted nor believed that you could go through this, you would have anticipated events and made choices that would have produced a different outcome.

And in doing so, you would have attracted other situations to go through. But this is the situation that you have attracted, and now is the moment to let yourself experience it.

Would you like some advice?

Do not run away. Let yourself go through what you need to go through, learn from the experience, and then move on to something new.

Use this opportunity to experience things to the fullest, to go as far as you can possibly go. This situation is now your mentor. It is here that you will learn. It is here that you will evolve.

And when the torment is over, when you have learned the lesson, look up to the sky, and you will see that another star has been placed there in your honor. And I will follow you, protecting you wherever you go.

JESUS

22

A Good Choice

Our essence is the core part of each of us. Our essence is that part of "us" that we place in things. In the things we do, in the things we think, and, above all, in the things we choose.

What does making the right choice mean?

People are always caught up in what is right and wrong.

To make the right choice means to choose things that are in harmony with our essence—without thinking about anything else, without considering other possibilities, without analyzing anything.

Just this—and this alone.

A choice made in harmony with our essence is always beneficial, because it embodies what we are in spirit.

A good choice may reflect how you are in your essence. And as such, regardless of the consequences, it is a choice in which you evolve.

A bad choice is one that is made for a number of reasons, none of which takes into account your essence. Obviously, when this happens, we, up in heaven are unable to protect you. It is *contra naturam* (against nature).

The answer to the question that brought you here is as follows: Where is your essence, that most profound part of you, your most intense feeling?

Close your eyes, think about the issue that is troubling you, and ask yourself these questions:

"Where would I place all of my heart and feelings today? Where would I place my essence?"

If the answer is "Here," then you may move ahead.

JESUS

23

Abundance

The original path is always one of abundance. If you do not find yourself in a situation of abundance, it means one of two things: either that you are not on your original path or that something is wrong with the course you have taken.

If this is the case, stop. Meditate, elevate yourself. There is almost certainly something that is holding you back. You are not acting in accordance with what you believe in. Your thoughts and deliberations are blocking you. You are not free. You are not completely free.

You must learn the following:

The ego makes you believe what it considers to be most opportune, in things that make life easier for you and do not cause you to be rejected.

The term "politically correct" was invented for this reason.

Political correctness is about conforming to thoughts and beliefs that are part of mainstream society and do not, therefore, cause offense or lead you to be rejected by other people or society itself.

This way, you will be accepted, integrated into society—and live imprisoned forever. Imprisoned because being "politically correct" is not who you are. Imprisoned because you are not able to think, believe, or act in accordance with your true self.

And so, energetically deformed, you continue to make your way, happily toward the cliff's edge.

It is obvious that you will end up attracting only loss. It is obvious that you will end up attracting only restrictions.

The path to freedom is the path to abundance.

Dare to be who you really are. And your life will shine twice as brightly because of the boldness you have shown.

JESUS

24

Acceptance

What was the reason we came to earth?

To procure and accumulate material possessions? To have a profession? To obtain power? To gain status?

None of these.

We came to earth to process our emotions, so that we may feel things.

We came to earth to experience everything, to experience both sides of duality, some of which are more pleasant than others.

Why are we taught that suffering is good for us?

Is it because we are meant to suffer?

No. It is because we accept all the good situations that we go through, but tend to reject those situations that are not as good (the ones we cannot change) but that we also need to experience.

In reality, the lesson that needs to be learned is not that suffering is good but that we need to accept and go through the experience of unhappiness in exactly the same way that we accept and experience happiness.

Only when you are willing to experience the two extremes of the same concept are you able to bring that subject to a close and move on to the next stage.

You should therefore accept every experience that is put before you, regardless of what this experience may be. If you are not able to change the direction of events, remain as you are, do not run away from the pain. Do not run away from suffering, accept it. Let yourself experience it.

Allow yourself to feel things to the fullest. Let yourself cry if necessary.

Only by doing this will you be able to put this behind you and continue on your journey.

JESUS

25

Commitment

When a man does what he has to do, this is called commitment.

When a man chooses to take on his heavenly responsibilities, such as being who he is and knowing himself well enough to choose in accordance with what he came to earth to do, rather than indulge his material responsibilities, which only cause him to distance himself from who he is, this is called commitment.

Your commitment is to me, this superior entity of sacred origin, and to all those who protect and guide you from heaven above.

But it is also to yourself, to your deepest being who speaks to you and with you so intimately about its fears and passions.

This is your commitment:

You will learn how to honor this, so that your presence on earth can be meaningful.

You will learn how to fulfill each part of the pact we made, where you agreed to honor the pure energy of heaven while down there in the midst of the earth's density.

You have never stopped believing.

You have never stopped existing.

You have always chosen to listen to the voice of intuition, which today reveals where you will be in a moment in time that you will never reach.

This wise voice that guides you on your journey will become clear only once the deal is sealed. Once you have pledged your commitment.

I am waiting for you up here.

Meditate.

Together, we vow that you will never again speak out or raise your hand to say anything or do anything that is in conflict with who you really are.

JESUS

26

Plenitude

Plenitude is the art of drifting through the heavens. It is the art of letting density drain away and then ascending. It is an art, probably the most sublime of all the arts. Artists should probably practice this a little more . . . then again, maybe they shouldn't.

It is a choice, always something that you choose.

Plenitude is the space we create inside ourselves in order to learn how to fly, to fly to wherever life takes us.

Plenitude is a being that is whole and magical. Plenitude is the harmony that exists between all things, including the ego and instinct. It is when duality wins and everything is harmonized.

It is when you have fulfilled the day's mission and can add this day to what you have already achieved.

Plenitude is when you hear a dog barking, a child crying, yet you do not move from that place deep inside where you have found your true self.

Plenitude is carrying on with the world as God made it.

It is floating on a buoy toward infinity, to take fresh news to heaven.

"Here we move along, carrying out the things we agreed to do. Each one does his bit."

We do ours.

We hope that it works out, that it ends successfully, so that you can soon be one of us. Plenitude is knowing that you, one day, will become a being of light again and you will be happy to return home.

Plenitude is knowing that one day time will end and we will be ready for the next journey.

All in good time.

It is still a long way off.

But we have already begun preparing for the feast.

JESUS

27

Self-esteem

Things are not always what they appear to be. What at first seems right for you may turn out not to be the experience your spirit is being prepared for down there on earth. There are questions you must ask:

What motivates me?

Why do I want to do this particular thing?

Why do I feel alone?

Why do I want to be accepted? Why do I want to be valued?

Now is the right time to ask yourself these types of questions.

Nothing that others give you, whether it be attention, acceptance, recognition, appreciation, or status—attributes that come from outside of yourself—can ever fill that enormous void within you:

Your lack of self-esteem.

And so you keep trying in vain to please those around you, hoping that their gratitude and acknowledgment will help you to increase your self-love and self-esteem.

Let's get this straight, once and for all.

How you feel about yourself, in other words your self-esteem, is not determined by what others may say, do, or give you. It is not determined by what you can achieve or gain, it is not determined by anything you can earn or pursue.

Self-love and an increase in self-esteem are determined by a number of factors that always come from the inside out, never the other way around. How you feel about yourself has more to do with being rather than doing or having.

Being is simple. It means being still and quiet and reaching down into the deepest part of your being. Feeling over and over again until you internalize what it is that you feel.

At first it will feel strange, but you will get used to it. It is, after all, a completely uninhabited place. But slowly, as you stop your thoughts and reach into yourself, to the very center of your feelings, you will finally begin to understand what "being" means.

To be is to feel. The rest is a song and dance that the ego does in order to distance you from what you are, from your inner self, which is where your essence lies.

Your self-esteem lies in being.

Everything you try to do or obtain to gain self-esteem will be pointless and ineffective, and you will only end up disillusioned, frustrated, and constantly in doubt.

Once you reach who you truly are, the unconditional love from above will, as if by magic, penetrate your life.

And if you already believe that heaven is magical, this will only reinforce that belief.

Come and meet me. Come and meet yourself.

JESUS

28

The Force

Man's strength is subjected to the forces of heaven.

Man needs to learn that without our energy, he is nothing. It is no use tugging on the rope, for it will always pull in the direction of the strongest side.

If what you intend to do has the force of the Universe behind it, that is wonderful.

It will all run smoothly, everything will flow, things will move along with the currents.

It will seem as if they are moving by themselves.

If what you intend to do has only your force behind it, then . . .

Who do you think you are, trying to take on all the forces within the Universe all by yourself?

If the Universe decides not to collaborate with you, it is far too heavy for you to push it alone.

Ask heaven to help you. And let heaven help you.

You should go where the wind goes.

If you notice that things are not moving on their own, then don't go any farther.

Do not try to force the future. It is there, already waiting for you, and it will not change direction just to please you.

JESUS

29

The Path

All paths lead to the sea. But there is only one path to happiness, and it is unique and special. The best way to recognize the path you should be on is to connect to the deepest part of your being and to work through your emotions. With each new discovery comes indescribable tranquility and inner peace.

But when man follows his own animal instinct, he wants nothing more than to meet his own needs so that he can be accepted, obtain power, and achieve even more.

He does this not for his own well-being but to be accepted externally.

The need to be accepted by society should not take precedence over your self-acceptance.

We all wish to be accepted. Being accepted by others is of great importance, but not as important as accepting ourselves.

No matter which path you wish to follow, the original path is the only true path.

Until this original path appears, you may continue to pursue other paths, but do not follow them with confidence or conviction.

These are simply paths you must follow, but they are not *the* path.

Be careful. Don't confuse these with the true path you are meant to take.

There is but one original path, and you know you have found it when your legs begin to shake, your heart beats hard, and your emotions surface. Your body will let you know when you have found it; you just need to pay attention to the signs.

Until then, until your body jumps for joy, crying out "It is here that I feel at home," travel these different paths, learn from them, but do not let yourself be mislead.

JESUS

30

Dissatisfaction

When a person feels dissatisfied, he feels in his heart that something is not quite right. There is always an underlying feeling of uncertainty.

It is a feeling of wanting, a feeling that something is not complete and that you need to find what is missing. And so off you go, a gallant knight, in pursuit of the missing link, and you do not rest until you have found it, even if it takes thousands of years.

This feeling that something is always missing overshadows everything.

This incessant need for plenitude, this attempt to feel good, is what makes that person run. And he does not rest until he has accomplished everything that he believes he must do.

This state of agitation, the feeling that there are things that always need to be done, is what causes people to be in constant movement, which in turn makes them feel even more dissatisfied.

The more a person does to avoid feeling dissatisfied, the more others will demand of him, given that he is the one person that is always on hand to do things. Yet this constant pressure brings more and more guilt and even greater dissatisfaction, for you can't do everything, can you?

And do you really have to do it all? Isn't it time to stop and look inside yourself to find the cause of your dissatisfaction?

This is not what plenitude is about. Plenitude doesn't run. It does not run ahead. It does not flee from inside itself. The person who is whole does not feel obliged to do things, because he knows that in order to be, he need only focus on being.

By not thinking about what there is to do, by concentrating on "being" rather than "what needs to be done," he unconsciously provokes others into doing things and this way remains free of burdens and of guilt.

To sum up: the more you concentrate on being and are able to recognize that you do not need to "do" in order to "be," the less others will demand of you, the less guilt you will feel, and the more you can focus on what it is that you most need right now, which is simply to be.

At this moment, feelings of guilt and urgency are crippling you. Detach yourself, cut your ties to matter, and just let yourself be. And watch how the world falls at your feet.

JESUS

31

Passion

Celebrate the sea, for it is part of who I am and what I know.

Whatever your passion is, for passion has no name, live each and every moment of it.

Whatever it is that you like to do, that you feel passionate about, do it.

Put as much of your heart into it as you can. Do it with passion, with the same amount of feeling that you put into something that you consider to be worthwhile.

When you come across a man watching over the sea so it does not become contaminated or claim any more victims, you will see how truly dedicated he is and how seriously he takes this task. He is never careless. He lives life to the fullest. This is where his deepest passion lies.

And now your turn.

Do something passionately.

Put your heart and soul into whatever you do, even the simplest of tasks.

It doesn't matter what you choose, but you must choose something. Just like the man who chooses to watch over the sea.

Choose something, and then put all of who you are into it. Give it your all. Make it everlasting. Place all that invisible force that comes from within, and that we call life, into it. Place all this into that action.

Decide what it is you want to do, and commit yourself completely to it.

It is in that instant, in that moment full of promise, that your soul becomes whole.

In that precise moment, you "are."

He is who he is because he watches over the sea. Watching over the sea helps him be the person he is.

The choice he made and how he acts defines his being.

Just as it defines who you are being at this moment.

JESUS

32
Rejection

I am going to let you in on a secret.

Everyone has rejection karma.

Rejection is the most common karma that exists within the circle of karmas.

Nowadays, it is one of the main karmas that most people have or, more precisely, the karma that everyone has.

Those born today are here to experience this karma. Not only to experience it but, if possible, to surpass it.

However, this is not how things always work out. They are not always able to do this.

Let's take a closer look.

Think about how most people behave in today's society.

They strive to live up to other people's expectations.

If they believe that others expect them to be strong, they will act strong in every situation.

They are not strong. They pretend to be strong to please others.

And why do they have a need to please others?

So that they are not rejected, of course.

Rejection karma.

A person will do whatever it takes to avoid being rejected.

This is why people strive to live up to the expectations that others have of them.

Now imagine that a person decides to go through the experience of being rejected, and, on accepting to go through this experience, he stops trying to please others or stops trying to live up to other people's expectations of him.

Imagine that this person decides to own up to who he really is, stops trying to fulfill expectations, and simply chooses to "be."

To be, in all plenitude.

What will happen next?

Alone and abandoned by others, this person will finally look at himself and understand the fear, the huge fear that lies within his heart.

It is this fear that needs to be cleansed. This is the mission.

To cleanse this fear so that we can finally cleanse the karma of rejection.

We need to accept rejection, to feel, to deeply feel the pain of not being liked, of not being accepted, to feel this pain and then to cleanse it whenever it appears.

Afterward, as this darkness gradually passes, a great Being will emerge, a human being with so much love to share with others.

Not a love that, out of fear of being rejected, tries to live up to all expectations, but a love that is free, profound, and unconditional, because it belongs to someone who has found his soul for all eternity.

JESUS

33

Dilution

What is a spiritual process?

What does it mean to go through a process?

To go through a spiritual process means to allow yourself to dilute in the waters.

Dilution is a powerful command from the soul.

The soul dilutes in the Universe. It dilutes in energy.

And it is through dilution that the soul becomes part of the whole, a part of the Universe.

The secret of communion lies in this act of dilution.

Because of how they act and live in density, there on earth, human beings are not in the slightest way ready for dilution.

They believe they are matter, they do not know they are energy.

If only they knew they were energy, for matter is just an outer layer that serves to support a person's physical limitations to working on his or her weaknesses . . .

If only they knew that their energetic side is their powerful side . . .

If only they knew that physical and spiritual dilution is the only way in which they will discover the dimension of their soul and finally be able to fuse . . .

If only they knew that the agreement they signed before incarnating requires them to dilute in energy so that they can successfully achieve the fusion that will give them back their unity . . .

If only they knew . . .

And how do you dilute in order to match the frequency of your soul?

It is easy:

To dilute means to allow things to happen when it is time for them to happen.

It is to know that there is a favorable time in the Universe and that people should not block things that are about to take place.

For example, if someone you like hurts you, allow yourself to cry over this. Cry through sadness. Cry because you have attracted a person who is so unhappy that he is willing to hurt those who care about him. That is all.

Only by doing this will you dilute in the emotions that you are feeling. Never, ever block out your pain.

You will gradually begin to get used to the idea that life brings you moments of joy and sadness, and if you are aware of these emotions, they will flow easily.

Feel, feel, feel.

But most people do not do this. They do not allow themselves to dilute into adverse emotions.

They become angry and enraged, they blame others, and they become hard, moving through life with their heart in knots because of these emotions that they refuse to accept.

As I always say, you do not have to accept the fact that others hurt you, but you do need to accept that you must go through the emotions that these experiences stir up in you.

Yet you go through one life after another refusing to feel, refusing to go through your emotions, never diluting.

And in doing so, you never reach the dimension of the soul.

You are never able to free yourself of matter.

And you never ascend.

JESUS

34

Friendliness

Friendliness is a sign from a higher plane. To be friendly means to emanate the energy of acceptance in another person's direction.

Everything that is accepted transforms into positive energy.

Anytime a dense energy receives acceptance, it either dissolves or is dislodged.

When this happens, all turmoil disappears, only peace remains.

Anger is energy without acceptance, peace is energy with acceptance.

At each event in your life, at each setback, ask yourself: Where am I failing to vibrate in acceptance? What do I still need to accept? What do I need to transform?

It is the ego that fails to accept.

Yet from the moment that energy is transformed, the heart opens up and receives so much love that you will inevitably need to share it with others.

This is what you, down there, call friendliness.

It is when a person has shed his load, accepted his limitations, mourned his loss, opened up to the heavens, received love, and now just emanates friendliness.

He simply emanates. Treating each person who crosses his path as a soul.

And when souls go hand in hand, the journey becomes much easier.

JESUS

35

Evolution

The real meaning of evolution does not lie in sadness.

It is not in suffering, joy, abundance, or restriction.

The real meaning of evolution cannot be found in any simplistic description of human emotions.

The real meaning of evolution is in evolution itself.

And given that evolution has no form or word, has no boundaries, and is overlooked by most people . . . the real meaning of evolution is what it is and when it happens.

It cannot be confined to a specific time or to any one sentiment.

It cannot be labeled in any way.

Thus, to reach the true meaning of evolution, we have to identify the feelings we need to work on.

These feelings have a name, they can be measured and verbalized and are very real.

Sadness is one of them. Every time I feel extremely sad, I am faced with a feeling that I need to work on.

And why sadness?

Rage is not a means to evolution. But sadness is.

Hate is not a means to evolution. But sadness is.

Guilt is not a means to evolution. But sadness is.

So what must you do? You must transform everything into sadness.

We tend to direct our rage at something or someone. However, you must be able to understand that you alone are responsible for everything that happens to you in life and that you attract each of your life experiences as a way of getting in touch with your sadness and unblocking the emotional karma you bring with you from another life . . .

If you are able to grasp these fundamental laws, you will come to understand that rage, hate, and guilt are basic emotions that you normally direct toward others so as to avoid dealing with your own sadness.

Once you are aware of this, you begin to transform rage, hate, and guilt into complete sadness. A sadness that is completely unadulterated.

And in doing so, you begin to arrive at the true meaning of evolution.

Sadness in its purest form is magical. It is alchemy. It changes lives, and it changes people.

Sadness reaches deep into the karmic knot and frees it. Only pure sadness, the emotion that has freed itself from rage, fear, violence, and density, is truly liberating. After sadness everything seems different.

Once a person has experienced as much pain as he can bear, he is free. He will no longer fear pain. He will no longer feel rage, for rage is a way of avoiding the pain that sadness creates.

He will no longer feel hate, for hate is a way of avoiding the pain that sadness creates.

He will no longer feel fear, guilt, jealousy, loneliness, or anxiety.

He will never feel anything other than sadness. And according to the theory of opposites, after restriction—if this is appropriately experienced—comes abundance.

After sadness come peace, joy, and happiness.

Take note.

You do not have to seek sadness. Be joyful whenever you can.

But if your heart is wounded, hurt, or in pain. If it is strained or even slightly torn, then stop whatever you are doing.

And whatever form this pain takes—for in order to prevent you from feeling pain, your ego will try to make you believe that it is others who have hurt you or that you have hurt yourself—let yourself experience it.

In that moment, everything will stop.

Remain alone with your sadness. Put others aside. Forget what you or they ought to have done.

Just let yourself feel sad.

Just let yourself feel sad.

Upon feeling sad, you accept freedom, you accept pain, and you accept life as it is.

You accept reality.

You accept evolution.

JESUS

36
Light

We cannot see only that which we want to see. We cannot live an illusion.

We have to face reality. We have to see things as they are.

That is why I like people who ask "for light" when they pray.

Enlighten me, so that I may clearly see things for what they are.

Give me light

That light where angels live,

That light which lights the way,

The light that transforms men

And makes them special.

Give me light

That light that stops me from feeling strange

And restores my true nature.

That light which lights up my steps

And gives me back a meaning to life, a sense of direction.

That light at the end of the tunnel,

Which offers a whole range of possibilities,

And an entire universe of opportunities.

That light, the color of peace, the color of a nation

That light that lives in heaven,

And gives greater meaning

To my life here on earth.

When you are feeling sad, remember that you may be in need of light. Say this prayer with an open heart, so that the light may enter and change your life.

JESUS

37

Communication

What is more important to you?

To say what needs to be said or to try to get another person to understand what it is that you are trying to say?

To express your point of view without a second thought as to how it may hurt others?

Think about it: When you simply fire your opinions at others, you are not taking into account that they will then become defensive or close down because you have hurt them. They simply stop listening to you and no longer understand what you are saying.

I keep on telling you that you have to be who you are, without deviations or concessions.

But in order to be your true self, you need to get others to understand you. That way you avoid creating misunderstanding, intolerance, and violence around you.

So this is the challenge: Be who you are with all your heart.

Next, use your mind to communicate this to others in a way that will help them to understand and accept you.

If they understand, great, for it will make it easier for you to be yourself.

If they still do not understand you, after all your efforts and diplomacy . . .

If they continue to wish you were different . . .

Then it is time to slam your fist down on the table and show them that you are not going to stop following the path that your soul lays before you each day.

JESUS

38
Desire

Have you noticed that the majority of people always want something?

"What I really want right now is to find a house like this or like that."

"I want to do this or that, this way or that way."

And when things don't happen, people tend to reinforce this "desire": "I would really like . . ."

They believe wholeheartedly that "you get what you wish for," and they "want" things in a way that is both violent and radical.

Answer me this:

If "you get what you wish for," why is it that what they "really wish for" isn't happening? Why don't people just stop for a moment to think about why they aren't getting the things they wish for?

It's simple. They want things to happen to them because they are not happy in the situation that they find themselves in.

So the ego "designs" a plan: if this thing happens to me, then I can get out of this situation. And that's it, the strategy is mapped out. From now on all you need to do is really "wish" for something.

What if I told you that this experience of discomfort was sent to you by the Universe and that you should let yourself experience it rather than run away from it?

What if I told you that your pain and discomfort will not go away until you are ready to go through this experience and allow yourself to hurt and cry when necessary?

And what if I told you that you will not resolve things until you accept this discomfort?

What if I told you that even if you choose to experience this discomfort, what comes after may not be at all what you expected?

Think about it.

JESUS

39

Forgiveness

We still need to forgive.

There is still a need for forgiveness.

But forgiveness is no small matter; to forgive is crucial, it is awkward, it is difficult, and it is indestructible.

Forgiveness requires understanding.

To forgive, you need to understand both sides.

And you have to forgive both sides.

You cannot forgive others unless you can forgive yourself.

And no one forgives himself unless he feels he has been forgiven by me; only someone who has experienced the powerful and liberating feeling of forgiveness, only someone who uses heaven to free himself from guilt, is able to forgive himself and then go on to forgive others.

All the rest is make-believe.

You may think you have forgiven. You may even act as if you have forgiven.

You may even openly say that you have forgiven, but until you have freed yourself from guilt by virtue of heaven, until you have completely forgiven yourself and understood that everything that has been done to you or that you have done is part of the plan . . .

. . . That intelligent and sacred plan that your life is comprised of . . .

If all these factors do not come together, then how are you able forgive anyone?

How can you relieve someone of his guilt?

The person who forgives, who knows how to come up to heaven to receive forgiveness . . . who is not always depriving himself of things because he believes he does not deserve them or should not accept them . . . who can feel deep down in his heart the energy of unconditional love in which "I love you for who you are, for everything you have done, and for everything that has been done to you. I love your soul" . . .

The person who is able to reach this point of evolution will know how to love a soul that is not his own, he will know how to forgive and to love unconditionally.

Love not only who that person is but, above all, who that person has chosen to be.

For you can forgive someone only when you are able to love the choices he has made.

Without judgment.

As you can see, forgiveness is not the beginning of the process. Forgiveness is the end.

JESUS

40

Crying

Crying is how we acknowledge our powerlessness. It is how we let go of our defenses. It is the way we accept our helplessness.

When you cry, you are accepting that there are things you cannot do. You are accepting that the things you desire may not be destined for you, at least not for now.

There are things your ego wants. It wants you to have what you wish for; it wants you to have possessions; it wants things to happen how and when you want them to. Deep down, the ego is searching for comfort.

The soul does not do this. It knows that each time things work out the way we want them to, we gain more defenses, increase our density, and start to lose our connection.

Things may actually happen as we desire. However, if they do, it is because they are "meant" to happen, because they are meant for us, and because it is the appointed spiritual time.

If this is the way it is, that's great. It means that your desire is connected to your soul and in line with the Universe. But if it is not, if you are projecting desires that are not fulfilled, then you have to:

Be aware that it is not the right spiritual time for what you desire to happen.

Be aware that your desires are a way of escaping your inner discomfort.

Allow yourself to cry over your inner discomfort, so as to be able to set it free.

If you complete these three stages, your experience will have been worthwhile. Your loss will have meaning.

As you know, to cleanse karma is to give meaning to your suffering, to learn why you had to lose. Karma is cleansed when you have completed all three stages.

Through crying, you will gain greater awareness.

You gain greater awareness when you get in touch with your emotions, and when you cry you are connecting to your emotions.

Cry.

But do not cry in anger, just because things did not happen "as you wanted them to." If they did not happen this way, it is because they were not meant to be.

Instead, allow yourself to cry because you are sad that they did not happen, that your time has not yet arrived.

Do not victimize yourself, crying because you believe others are evil or because they have hurt you.

No one has hurt you. We attract everything that happens to us.

You need to understand what kind of energy you are emanating, so that you may understand why you are attracting this.

Instead, cry over the fact that you are emitting density, displeasure, rage, or anger, or simply because you are emitting an energy that does not belong to you.

Simply cry. To cry does not, as many believe, signify that you attract negative energies. To cry is to expel the negative energy that is in your heart.

It may have been there for centuries; maybe today it will finally have the opportunity to release itself.

Cry.

And be happy.

JESUS

41
Spiritual Dimension

Everyone has a secret side. A hidden side, a part of him that lies latent.

A place buried deep within, where only those who believe in their cosmic existence may enter, where only those who are attentive, fragile, and defenseless may enter.

Entry is permitted only to those who wish to get in touch with their feelings, regardless of the inherent risks involved; to those who are willing to accept the unknown; to those who accept pain in all its magnitude, just as they accept light as it transcends; to those who accept absolute duality, and only to those who accept that good and evil are part of the same sphere and do not yearn for days of happiness when faced with pain.

These days will arrive once you have gone through the pain.

Every person has a spiritual dimension. In order to access this, you have to cleanse your thoughts, put on some music, and be.

Simply be.

Just remain there, listening to music and letting it vibrate through the foundations of life. That is to say, through yourself, without thinking, without feeling. Only being.

And a magnetic gateway will open up a whole new world of awareness. Remain in this world. Stay there and build, gather, and strengthen that vibration.

And as each day passes, you will find it easier to access, to remove all thoughts from your head, and to simply vibrate.

Just be.

This is only the beginning.

JESUS

42
Unconditional Love

Today we are going to talk about unconditional love.

It is the forbidden love. It is the love that everyone yearns for, that everyone wishes to touch.

It is the love that is interested in neither what you believe in nor the way you behave, nor in your status, religion, circumstances, or surroundings.

It is an unmitigated love, a love without fear and without judgment. It has no memory or feelings of revenge.

It is absolute love.

It simply loves, and that is all. It loves for no other reason than to love. It loves without reservations.

No matter who you are, no matter what you do, what consequences you attract, or how you live your life, I will always be here.

Always ready, always whole, loving you as you are.

For the way you choose to be in this lifetime.

My love is not conditional, there are no restrictions. I only love.

This is my way of protecting you, guiding you, understanding you, and enlightening you.

Life teaches you lessons, and I love you. Together, life and I work side by side to guide you through your passage on earth.

Open up your heart. Let my love enter. Only when you have received my unconditional love and feel protected by heaven can you emanate love. Emanate self-love, which will inevitably allow you to forgive yourself and accept yourself as you really are—emanate love toward others, which in its turn will bring more love—emanate love toward the earth and animals, which will prolong human beings' stay on earth.

Open up your heart. Reconnect with your feelings.

Just for a while, stop thinking, running, and flying without any sense of direction or meaning.

Stop. Look into your heart and open it up.

Let me inside, slowly, one step at a time. Let me enter and remain there.

And you will see how everything becomes clearer. How everything transforms into light.

And I will have one more reason for being here. And that reason is you.

JESUS

43

Restriction and Abundance

Nature is abundant.

There is a great amount of water, many trees, flowers, and plants.

There are so many fish, so many different species, so many people, and so much land.

The earth is vast, and if its resources are used correctly, there is plenty for everyone.

People can literally have it all.

So why don't they?

Although it is not easy to understand this, the truth is that human beings do not have what they need because they vibrate through restriction.

The following explanation may make it easier to understand:

Human beings do not have because they are afraid of not having.

It seems ironic, doesn't it? But it is true.

Even the most powerful men are afraid of losing their power.

So they grab on to it at all costs and end up losing sight of their initial goal.

No sooner have men acquired material wealth than they change vibration. They start being afraid of losing their possessions.

They may even die rich, but the fear they feel in their heart, that feeling of insecurity, begins to eat away at their emotional cells. They die rich. But they die afraid. They feel anguished throughout their entire life.

They attempt to hold on to what they have. But it is easier to obtain something than to hold on to it.

And what of those who have nothing?

They want to have things. They fight, struggle, humiliate, and emit restrictive energy.

Those who have nothing want something.

Those who have something want to hold on to it.

Pure restriction.

And because of this, men fight, men mistreat one another, and men humiliate one another.

Pure restriction.

Life is an ode to nature. Life pays homage to life itself.

You have to understand that nothing belongs to you, that everything life lends you is to be lived, used, and enjoyed as much as possible, regardless of whether it is good or bad.

Do not try to get anywhere, just enjoy being who you are, and if possible, be happy, and if not, process all your pain so that it may quickly disappear and a new day can begin.

Do not flee from your sorrows. Let yourself cry over them and grieve for each day and each situation so that you can move forward.

Do not put your feelings on hold.

Do not leave anything behind.

Your chest will become cleansed.

Your heart will become calmer.

Your emotions will become clearer.

The tears you cry will then give way to a radiant smile.

To stop vibrating through restriction is to know that each day is unique and will never repeat itself. And today is always a great opportunity for living.

And if you live today well, tomorrow will be even better.

JESUS

44

Taking Risks

Fear of making mistakes. This is where the problem lies.

Everyone has a fear of making mistakes. And because of this they do not take risks, they do not grow, and they do not fly.

When you take risks, you learn, let down barriers, and gain self-confidence, even if you do make mistakes.

And if you do make mistakes, you just count your blessings, deal with your sadness, tend to your wounds, and give yourself time to grieve.

To err is to learn. To err is to grow.

Does it hurt? Of course it hurts. No one likes to fail. But if nobody ventured out through fear of failing, what type of world would we live in?

If explorers had feared the sea, maritime disasters, storms, and monsters, what would the world be like today? There would be but a handful of countries and very little else.

Take a risk. Take a risk, and put all your heart into it. Do it out of love.

Do not take risks for personal gain, just because you will receive things.

Take risks because your soul is pleading for you to move forward, because your intuition tells you to do so at an energetic level.

Venture out and go in search of the new world, which is available only to those who devoutly believe that they can fly.

JESUS

45

Freedom

Freedom is magical. It makes you feel as if you have done what needed to be done, that you are where you need to be, and that everything is in its place.

Freedom is not a place. You do not have to go anywhere. You do not have to do anything in order to be free.

To be free is to be aware that life is yours and yours alone, and that you should live it to the fullest and be who you are without making concessions.

Obviously, you may take others into consideration, but you must set boundaries. There are people who live solely for others.

Everything they do, they do for others. They live their lives to please other people.

These people are constantly making concessions in their lives.

They strive to live up to other people's expectations.

And once the pressure becomes unbearable, they desperately seek freedom in a vain attempt to find themselves.

Yet they always look for freedom outside of themselves, by running away from who they are.

They set off in search of freedom.

I do not go anywhere in order to be free.

The most I can do is go, because I am free.

Only when you have inner freedom may you go on to do what you wish, for everything that you do will inevitably reflect the person you already are.

And what is inner freedom?

It is living each emotion to the fullest, however insignificant it may seem.

Feel who you are, and do not make concessions.

Feel, feel, feel. This feeling will provide you with precious spiritual knowledge about who you are and what you came to earth to do.

Feel, open up your heart, and follow your intuition.

Then, and only then, act on it.

Once you are on this path, you will find the most fabulous way of being free.

JESUS

46

The Joy of Liberation

Fear binds you. Fear restrains you. It prevents you from moving forward.

No matter how hard you try, you simply cannot move.

Fear limits you. And fear is huge. It is gigantic.

It invades everything. It destroys. Every time you want to move ahead, fear appears.

That hateful fear. It brings everything to a standstill. It blocks everything.

And you begin to live in function of your fear. Because you are afraid to go here, you go there instead. Because you are afraid to do this, you do that instead.

You stray from your original path. And life becomes blocked.

Nothing seems to work out. Nothing flows. It seems as if time has stopped. Nothing seems to make sense anymore.

A life lived outside of its original path is a life devoid of meaning.

And so what do you do now? How can you stop this blockage?

How can you free yourself?

There is only one answer, and it is simple: Let yourself feel the fear. Let the fear grow within your chest. Let it invade everything and become huge, gigantic.

When it is big, very big, ask for a beam of light and begin cleansing. The beam will slowly vaporize the fear, taking that huge amount of karmic density with it.

I know that it is difficult. But it is also difficult to live with that fear. To live in fear.

And gradually, this monster will begin to disappear.

The clouds will disappear so that the sun may return.

And you will gradually begin to feel calmness, tranquillity, and harmony.

When this happens, you will understand where it is that you have been, invaded by fear, so far from the light.

And you will realize that it is possible to change things, you will understand that there is another life to be lived, one that is more tranquil, happier, and lighter.

And fundamentally purer and more enlightened.

And at this point you will understand the joy of liberation.

And you will agree that life is a gift and truly worth living.

JESUS

47

The Gift

Whenever the Universe creates loss, whether it is economic loss, material loss, physical or emotional loss, it is actually offering you something: a connection.

A connection with heaven so that you may understand why you had to attract this loss and what type of energy you are emanating that results in loss. Second, it offers you the chance to connect with your emotions. Spiritually, a loss signifies suffering, not anger, and when you attract loss, you should simply cry over it. Grieve for what you have lost. Then let it go, with suffering, with pain.

The pain of detachment will increase your sensitivity; make you feel more connected to your emotions.

It will make you feel more fragile and on edge, more "thin-skinned," as the saying goes.

It will heighten your sensitivity.

And heightened sensitivity is a gift.

To sum up: you attract loss so that you can become more sensitive, more fragile, and more intuitive, and so that you may use this gift.

From this we can deduce that the Universe reharmonizes only that which is not in harmony, and when it sends you loss as a way of making you more sensitive, it is because you were emanating the opposite of this.

It is likely that you were emanating total disconnection, being defensive and irrational and trying to prove you are strong. All these things are incompatible with the spiritual being.

A piece of advice:

If you are able to remain sensitive and fragile, intuitive and connected, if you can hold on to this gift, the Universe will no longer need to reharmonize anything and will never again send you loss.

Do you want to give it a try?

JESUS

48

Inside and Outside

There are only two ways to live: connected or disconnected.

Deeply connected to who we are, to what we came here to do, to the different ways in which we can outwardly express our being.

But in order to express who we are, we first need to be. And in order to be it is essential to look deep within ourselves so that we may understand what we are feeling, what it is that is hurting, what makes us happy and unhappy, where our freedom and conscience lie, what hurts us, what makes us feel bad, and what it is that elevates us.

As you can see, everything happens on the inside.

Everything you do reflects your inner state.

If things are not working out for you, if your actions are not effective, it is because they are not reflecting your inner world.

They are simply reflecting an evasive inner world, which is both confused and disconnected. This is why our actions do not work out; they are products of our inconsistency.

You need to look within you and see what it is that you are running from. You have to face up to your demons, let yourself feel the pain, and, once everything is cleansed, get in touch with your soul, your essence.

Only when you have done this may you proceed.

Actions promoted by the soul are always and without exception correct, enlightened, and gratifying. This is the only way to evolution.

You may live another way: disconnected.

When you are disconnected, you do not know yourself, you flee from what you feel, and in order to avoid pain you take refuge in material possessions.

This results in loss, pain, frustration, and illness.

You always have a choice.

JESUS

49

Change

Is my belief system rigid? Do I ever change my mind? Once I have formed an opinion, do I exclude everything else?

I am "biased." Preconception, an idea formed beforehand . . .

A notion or opinion formed before you have gained an understanding of the issue at hand.

Our mind should be like the sky, studded with stars.

There is always something in motion. There is always a star shining, a galaxy in movement, a supernova exploding, a star that is dying, and so many others that are being born.

Nothing ever comes to a standstill, neither in the sky nor in your life.

Bear in mind that what exists today, may not exist tomorrow.

And what existed yesterday may—or may not—remain the same.

On the day your belief system finally admits that anything is possible, that anything can happen, your indigo chakra will open itself to an infinite number of opportunities.

And when your mind opens and elevates itself, you begin to express what you feel, rather than what you think.

You no longer need words to communicate, because a simple glance, touch, or smile can lead to a more valuable, intuitive, sacred, and eternal form of communication.

And with freedom of communication you intuitively know what to say and how to say it.

JESUS

50

Emotional Neediness

To be needy is both sad and unbearable, yet to run away from our emotional needs is even more frightening.

It is because of his emotional needs that man is defensive, self-destructive, and complicated. He asserts himself, gets angry, and lives in torment.

Man invented power in order to avoid being invaded.

It is because of power that man flees his violent need for love, understanding, and self-esteem.

Man asserts himself, man survives, and man flees from his emotions. He undervalues and minimizes his emotions.

In effect, man is putting on his purest mask, his ancestral mask, the mask of the "tough man" who can endure anything. The mask that is strong enough to move mountains, the mask that can win a thousand battles. The one that is fearless enough to wander across different countries and continents searching for a state of nothing-ness, for glory, success, or immortality.

And who knows what would happen if he stopped for a while and went in search of what he needs, his sensitivity . . .

If only he accepted that every flower is a world within itself and that each day that he lives is an opportunity created by the Universe . . .

Life is to be felt.

What is the use of great achievements if there is pain in your heart? If there is still a dangerous and malignant hole in your heart, a huge void that brings you down to earth, that brings you back to reality?

Pain. A void. The fear that this pain is everlasting and that this void will continue to spread.

When we are able to move toward the light, when we are willing to accept our emotions, our needs, our shortcomings, and every-thing that belongs to us, when we are able to accept that power will not provide us with what we need and that assertiveness does not cover this gaping hole, this neediness . . .

When we understand that the only remedy for this pain is to allow ourselves to hurt and to direct the light that enters through our head toward this hole . . .

When we have understood all this, then we are ready to begin changing.

When you are in pain, allow yourself to feel it. Open up your heart and allow the density to come out.

Stop trying to be better than others. Try to be more in touch with who you are. Not for others, but for your own original energy.

For your soul.

JESUS

51

Fear

Fear.

Survival.

Feel the fear. Feel the fear. Feel it deeply.

Let fear emerge.

Let yourself feel fear. This is the emotion that destroys your dreams, that does not allow you to believe.

It is this emotion that hinders your progress. Everything you do on your own and for yourself is annihilated.

You are afraid to die.

Only those who experience the fear of dying are able to value life. To know the blessing that life is.

Fear is the hidden enemy.

It is in the name of fear that great pacts are forged with dark forces.

It is in the name of fear that we wage wars that are both extravagant and capricious.

It is in the name of fear that we flee forever from our path.

The solution to fear is allowing yourself to feel the pain.

And the light that enters your mind will gradually cleanse that pain.

Allow it to enter, allow yourself to hurt, not because someone did something wrong, not because you did something wrong, but because of the deep sadness felt at knowing that this is how it must be.

Let yourself hurt.

And then come up to heaven to regenerate.

Come up to heaven to receive the light.

JESUS

52
Time

The present moment, the one we are living in now, may be perfect for some ventures but not for others.

It may be excellent for the development of some relationships but not for others.

It may be ideal for some creations or certain material investments but prove to be disastrous for others.

The secret is timing.

Whether or not the different elements in matter work together with the Universe depends on whether it is the right moment in time.

The smallest being has the capacity to live or die.

It is time that decides.

If men learn how to identify when the moment is right, they will know exactly when to move forward.

Those men who learn the secrets of time will know when to proceed.

Men possess a heart that sends them messages, that shows different paths, that shortens their journey.

Listen to yours.

JESUS

53

Attachment

Every day, life offers us the opportunity to reestablish priorities.

Every day, every hour, the Universe reharmonizes everything that is out of balance. Whatever is not centered is modified by the energetic system.

Whenever you believe you possess something, even if it is a subconscious thought, the Universe gets ready to take it away.

Even if are you not aware of it, you are constantly attaching yourself to something. And by doing so, you lose your freedom. You become chained to what you have attached yourself to. You can become attached to anything: to people, material possessions, ideas, ideals, judgments, words, or choices.

When you realize that you no longer want to let go, it means you have become too attached. When you think you will never suffer loss, it means that you have become too attached. And it is here that you become a prime candidate for loss.

You have to let go.

Every day, you are given the opportunity to free yourself. When you find yourself momentarily without money, it is a sign that you have to disconnect yourself from money. Those who do not heed the signs will never again have money.

When a child wishes to become independent, it is a sign that you have to begin to let him go. Those who do not heed the signs will end up losing their children.

When you feel sad, cry. Allow yourself to express your fragility.

Those who do not heed the signs will end up attracting illnesses, which are severe signs of fragility.

Give yourself permission to disconnect from things, from the idea that you have to be strong, that things belong to you.

These are losses that will hurt. It is true, they do hurt. But they prevent definitive loss.

They prevent life from being as hard on you as you are on yourself.

JESUS

54
Fate

All galaxies contain fields of electromagnetic energy that, for some reason, attract one another. This initial attraction is what delineates all future events.

When galaxies collide, it is because they were predestined to be united forever. This collision is simply a consequence of this.

They collided because they attracted one another, and then they stayed together. They did not stay together just because they collided. Can you see the difference?

In the first example, before they came into contact, the galaxies had already worked on attracting one another. The collision was a consequence of their hard work; staying together was fate.

Why am I explaining all this to you?

Because people are the same as galaxies.

When they run into each other or cross paths, it means that their fate was already outlined.

They had already attracted one another. The collision was simply the outcome of this.

Before colliding, the galaxies perform a drawn out and distant dance and, after many, many years, come together.

They had already expected to come together when they were drawn to one another. Staying together is a consequence of this attraction. It is not a consequence of their collision, given that there are some galaxies that collide and end up repelling each other.

It is the same with human beings. When you attract a person or situation in your life, you already feel through the frequency of the vibration whether the meeting will be to attract or repel.

Whatever the outcome, this meeting was planned centuries ago.

JESUS

55

The Present and the Future

I am going to tell you why it is so important for people to live in the present.

Not in the past or future but in the present.

To simply be in the present and experience what there is to experience, here and now.

Much has been said about living in the here and now.

But there are still things that need to be explained, things that need clarifying.

When you live in the past, all your energy vibrates in a frequency from the past.

If, in the past, you ever felt hate, anger, or guilt, that is to say, any of these basic instincts, these emotions from the past, will be channeled into the present. They will invade your life, given that the gateway to time is open and the different time dimensions now interconnect. Interact. Intertwine.

Because you insist on living and thinking only in the past you will be bombarded with conflicting emotions from the present.

Past emotions will begin to dominate the present, your life, and your energy. You will begin to live off your memories and turn into a sad human being without any energy, given that we only attract energy when we resolve something.

If you live in the present, you may revisit past memories, but you do so fully aware of the present. You go back to the past but with a broader, clearer, and cleansed consciousness.

And inevitably, when your age-old blocked emotions are forced to deal with your present consciousness, they dissolve into a million fragments of light.

You begin to live more peacefully, for you are living in a time dimension in which you can change events through your own free will. The choice is yours. Those who live in the past cannot change anything. The past cannot be altered. You live your life with an enormous sense of powerlessness, for you are living in a past that you cannot change, rather than in the present where you are able to change the course of events.

So now you have a clearer understanding of why you should not live in the past. You may return there with your present-day awareness, in order to free any blockages you may have, but you cannot live there.

Now let's talk about the future. Why is it necessarily a bad thing to live focused on the future?

People who are focused on tomorrow end up infinitely weaker.

They do not have energy from the present; they reject it in favor of events that have yet to happen, but since they cannot force these events to take place, it is more than likely that they will never materialize.

Because they live focused on the future, they do not care about, focus on, or devote themselves to the present.

And what do you think happens to those people who do not prepare for their future? To those who do not dedicate themselves to life so that great things may happen?

To those who do not take care of things so that they may grow?

What sort of future awaits those who do not focus on the present so that they may understand what it is they have to do and how to do it when it is time to take action?

Nothing whatsoever.

There will be no future.

Months and years may pass.

Time may pass, but that person's life will not change, nothing will change. He will continue to wait for satisfactory events to take place in a future that never arrives.

He will live in waiting . . .

Although these are already sufficient reasons for living in the present, I would like to give you an all-important reason for choosing the here and now.

I can enter only where there is consciousness.

I can enter only where there is total consciousness.

I can enter only when you invite me in.

When you make space for me to enter.

When your consciousness is focused on the heart, on what you feel, you allow me to come in peacefully.

A person who reveals his sensitive side, who accepts his difficulties and limitations as well as his abilities, and, even more important, who takes his own evolution in hand, choosing to live for today regardless of what it may bring, is someone who is calling out to me.

A long-lasting call that evokes an ancient friendship.

These people I approach.

Into them I enter.

But those who insist on living outside their time, whether it is in the past, where sorrows emerge, or in the future, where they believe anything can happen, are in no condition to let in the light.

They block. They resist. They control.

The only thing I can do for these people is wait.

And so I remain here, feeling sad and useless, watching them distance themselves from the light, watching them continuously distance themselves from me. Suffering alone and in complete spiritual solitude.

Remember that you need only feel in order to contact me.

To deeply feel any of the emotions that exist. Never judging or blaming others for what has happened in your life. Simply letting yourself feel, feel, feel.

And I will be here, looking up from above, making sure that as a result of your feeling so deeply, your emotional blockages will finally begin to dissolve and you may once again have hope and look up to the heavens.

JESUS

56
Negativity

Think about this:

Our experience on earth is the experience of negativity.

Though still made of light, human beings come down to earth, where there is negativity.

From the moment they are born they experience recurring situations of negativity. They go through the trauma of childbirth, are often brought up by overbearing parents, and are rejected by their peers and society, as well as the people who try to mold them. In short, negativity is present at every moment of our lives.

The question is:

How does a person react to all this negativity?

Does the person become negative?

As long as he remains negative, he will keep returning and attracting even more negativity.

However, there will come a day when this being decides to react to negativity by being positive. He receives negativity but does not allow it inside him. He remains in light. And when he no longer has negativity, he is ready to end his days in matter.

He will not reincarnate.

He will never again experience life on earth.

He has exceeded the experience of negativity and will depart for new domains.

JESUS

57

The Present Moment

The best way to connect with heaven is to live in the present moment.

It is a unique moment, and once it is over, it will never again return.

If you try to delay this moment, it will transform itself into the past.

If you try to anticipate it, trying to control what is going to happen, it will never be anything other than the future, a frequency of the future, for as you know, the absolute future does not exist.

People's free will should always be taken into consideration. It is the choices each of us makes that shape the future. What lies ahead is always a consequence of our past and present.

To sum up, live today, the here and now, this precise moment in which you can effectively make choices.

You cannot choose the past, for the past has already been chosen.

Your present has been shaped by choices made in the past.

What is important now is that you live today wisely and put into practice what you have chosen. Your choice will reveal who you truly are. If you live the here and now, if you live this moment with intensity, you will be so in touch with your own feelings and emotions that you will have no other option but to choose in accordance with these.

And so, you will build your future based not on suppositions but on the facts that reveal your true being.

And this future can be nothing other than prosperous and happy.

Do not forget:

To feel anguish and guilt is to live in the past.

To feel anxiety is to live in the future.

Live in the here and now, this moment, and you will be inspired to be who you really are.

JESUS

58

Traps

Problems are traps. Just think about it. Problems are nothing more than traps.

Let me explain.

Picture a being of light—you—experiencing density, experiencing negativity—life on earth.

Imagine that this being of light descends to earth with the sole intention of reacting to density.

It is his choice: he can react with light, which is who he truly is, or he can react by becoming dense, like the earth.

If he does become dense, he will be pulled toward density—earth—over and over again, until he learns his lesson and is able to maintain himself in light while in the world of density.

Obviously, at some point within these reincarnations, he will return to light. This being dies in matter and returns to light. To recycle, to remember who he was, to recall that he is light.

He then returns once more to earth to try to transcend this experience, to remain in light.

Throughout your life on earth, we continue to send you dense experiences—in reality it is beings that attract these experiences—problems, frustrations, injustices, betrayals. All extremely dense experiences aimed at testing your reaction.

Will this being remain in light and be true to himself, thus stepping out of the wheel of incarnations once his mission is accomplished? Or will he transform into density and continue to return to earth?

What will he choose?

Many beings try to alter density because they are unable to withstand this experience, this difficult test that they must go through.

They want the world to be just, to be perfect.

Well, if the world were just and perfect, you would no longer have to experience density.

A being would come to earth, and there would be no traps to test his reaction.

There would be nothing to choose between. Everything would be light. There would be light up here and light down there.

This doesn't make any sense. When we send you down there—or, more to the point, when you choose to go down to earth—it is precisely so that you can experience the traps that exist in dense matter and see if you are able to remain in light or whether you transform into materialistic, rational, and dense beings.

The problems you go through are nothing more than traps laid out by heaven to test your level of density and your level of light.

They are a way of testing your reaction to density.

The choice is yours.

JESUS

59

Minimalism

The Universe is what it is only because you are who you are.

Think about it.

The Universe has equilibrium, and each and every being that exists in the Universe, whether alive or not, is part of this equilibrium.

All energies are unique, and each being has to vibrate at the frequency of these unique energies.

When these unique energies come together, they complete the Universe as a whole.

If the whole of the Universe has been assembled by God, then God is the sum of all these unique energies. From this perspective, you can now see how each of you is a part of God, but only when you are vibrating in the frequency of your unique energy.

To vibrate through this unique and nontransmissible energy is what is currently known as being.

Being is this. It is to vibrate through your own energy, an energy that no one else has. And in order to vibrate through this energy, in the beginning, you have to be minimalist.

Minimalist in the sense that you take things to the minimum:

You are simply energy and nothing more. You neither think nor feel, you only vibrate through energy.

On removing all thoughts from your mind, on removing the density from your heart, you access your being. And you vibrate through it.

And from here onward, from this vibration, you will begin to do and think about things there in matter, about that which fully reflects who you truly are.

You will no longer do things in order to be or try to obtain things in order to be.

You will do and have because you are.

This changes everything.

When people down there are unable to vibrate simply through being, they tend to project outside themselves. They try to obtain and do things that will supposedly give them a sense of who they are.

People crave houses, cars, and good jobs because they believe they will make them feel that they are someone (the owner of a house or car, someone who has a good job), but this is not what being means. These people do not usually vibrate through who they are. In the majority of cases, the more material possessions people have, the more they vibrate through the fear they have of losing them.

Every time you desire something that is outside yourself, whenever you anxiously desire anything other than to simply vibrate through being, read this text again and try to understand that this desire just hides your dissatisfaction at not being able to vibrate through your own unique frequency.

Be minimalist, let go of your thoughts, remove the density from your heart, and simply exist. Many people believe that just existing gets you nowhere. That to simply exist is not enough, does not promote a state of being.

I tell you that to simply exist, to be minimalist, is probably the best energetic training a being can have.

Believe me.

JESUS

60

Consciousness

Think about consciousness. Think about how complex it is.

Think about how many neurons and atoms are needed to develop human consciousness.

If we had equipment that could measure consciousness, imagine how sophisticated it would need to be.

Think about this great Universe that you possess—an undeniably infinite Universe—when you bear in mind that beings of light are here to enlighten your consciousness.

Imagine how elevated your life would be if you really took advantage of the connection and allowed us to intervene in your lives in a clear and intelligible manner. In a way that is not only abstract and far-reaching but complete.

You would become such great men. You would go on to use the greatest weapon that human beings possess, consciousness. And alongside this, you would have the greatest tool for expansion, the connection to heaven, the open channel. The energetic opening to heaven that would allow you to choose, experience things, give meaning to what you experience, and then move forward.

Consciousness—an element that has been so greatly misunderstood.

In his desire to control, man continuously attempts to dominate his consciousness, training it to become more and more connected to matter, rather than detaching himself from it and allowing himself to connect to heaven.

I am here; I can help, but only if your minds and souls are open to receive me.

There is no way around a closed heart. You cannot revive it.

Your choice involves opening up your heart so that I can enter and carry out my plan.

I appear when your consciousness connects with me. I take hold of your life and do what I need to do. And you believe they are miracles taking place.

Miracles are nothing more than my intervening in matter.

Divine interventions, as you down there say.

But to enter, the divine needs an invitation.

It needs to be chosen, it requires an open heart.

First and foremost, before meditation and before elevation, you need to begin to open up. Open your heart. Look up to the sky and accept that I can enter if you let me, if you open up.

JESUS

61
Confusion

What really saddens me is when people get everything confused.

They confuse devotion with obligation. They confuse karma with sin. They confuse fear with austerity.

I want you to know that I have never demanded anything from any of you.

Whoever says otherwise is lying.

Whoever says that I defined obligations, whoever says that I was behind the prohibition of sins, is being untruthful about the order in which things took place.

I mentioned only concepts. I spoke of freedom, ignorance, transcendence, death, and the downfall of states.

I spoke of poignancy and eloquence. I spoke of the ego's death and the soul's life.

I spoke of distance, commitment, and abundance.

I never said anything whatsoever about obligations, prohibition, shame, hell, or punishment.

I never said anything to restrain the human soul. My words served to highlight, elate, and honor the soul.

When you put words into my mouth that only serve to diminish the human soul, I feel sad, futile, and misunderstood.

I almost find myself thinking that it wasn't worth the effort.

When you use me to mistreat, punish, and cause grief, when you use my name to satisfy your own desires and self-importance, I want to cry out that this is not the way.

This is why I ask:

That you think for yourselves.

That you draw your own conclusions.

If what they tell you I said does not have the frequency of freedom, light, and clarity, if what they say about me does not have the frequency of life, love, and the soul, please do not listen to them.

Do not allow fear to get the better of you.

Do not allow density to settle in.

When you begin to feel this, ascend; get in touch with your hearts. There is nothing in this world that can force you to believe in density.

There is nothing in this world that can prevent people from being happy.

JESUS

62
Yang

Yang is for fighting, but what are you fighting for? If I am always telling you to abandon your ego, if I am always asking you to reduce that *yang* energy, which is more proactive, more advanced, and more focused on struggle, if I am always asking you to moderate it, why does it exist in matter?

Why do men carry *yang* energy in equal proportion to *yin* energy, which is more placid, more spiritual, and more receptive?

Why does it exist with such intensity?

The answer is simple. Let me explain.

Man does not come to earth simply to be happy.

This is not what is expected of him.

Man comes to earth to work on himself. To work through his fears and his discomforts; in other words, to work on his limitations.

Each fear and each discomfort is an energetic block provoked by karmic memory. By the memory of a trauma suffered in another lifetime.

Each of these emotional blockages must be overcome. The man who is able to overcome these emotional blockages and does not accumulate any more within this lifetime is actually preparing to ascend.

So if a being comes down to earth to undo these blockages, what does he need to do?

He needs to experience them, live them, understand them and accept them. When he does this, when he really faces his difficulties, something begins to gradually change.

Once this being becomes aware of his fear, he removes the strength it had over him.

Hence, it is not difficult to guess what happens to people's fears when they decide to face them. They purely and simply start to disappear.

And where does *yang* come into this story? Where can you find strength, will, and sometimes even a little ego? In the decision to face one's fears. To face difficulties head-on and to work through them until they no longer hold any meaning.

Continuous verbal aggression will end up losing its power.

Once you have confronted your fear a few times, it too loses its power.

This sounds like the theory of pain, the idea that suffering is good for you, doesn't it?

There is, however, a huge difference. Until now, it was said that suffering made men honorable. Man suffered to be worthy. He believed that through suffering he would gain dignity. Notice how he is thinking from the outside in.

Man believed that the act of suffering would make him into a certain type of person.

But the truth is that things happen in the reverse order. First you are, and then you act in accordance with who you are. You don't become a certain person just because you behave in a certain way.

As I have said, these men suffered so they could become something, they worked from the outside in.

Today, when I ask you to face your pain, I am not asking you to make yourself suffer. I am asking you not to run away from pain. If it comes knocking on your door, I want you to face it.

I want you to go through it. I want you to allow yourself to feel the pain in the center of your heart, to go to the very depths of your pain without victimizing yourself and without feeling that others are to blame.

Acknowledge that you are responsible for it, that what you are going through is a consequence of your past life actions or emotions.

This is why we need *yang*.

This is why you need courage, the courage to show your fragility and to keep dealing with the pain until you stop hurting.

You stop hurting not because you have rationalized things and think it would be best to channel your energy elsewhere.

You stop hurting not because you have taken an antidepressant to numb the pain.

You stop hurting, not because you hide away from your own reality by praying endlessly to God to resolve your problems but because you have had the courage to stay, to let yourself feel the pain, to feel it so deeply that it becomes part of you.

Until one day it no longer exists, it scatters like a cloud, dissolves above the ocean. The pain came; you guided it, and it disappeared. This is what *yang* is for. This is why the ego exists. So that in the midst of darkness, you can fill yourself with light and say:

"I deserve to be happy. I like myself enough to choose to remain here, motionless, allowing the pain to completely engulf me, so that it can then leave me forever. I deserve to be happy. And when this pain is over, I know that I have conquered another place in heaven."

This is what courage is for.

The difference between experiencing a painful situation in the traditional form and in the spiritual form is as follows: in the traditional form, a person believes that he is a victim of fate, that he is being harmed for no apparent reason, and that he has no control over the situation. In the spiritual form, however, the person knows that if he is hurting, it is because he needs to work through things, so he tries to go through this experience over and over again until he reaches the point where he has dealt with the situation so many times that his heart opens and he overcomes his emotional blockages.

JESUS

63

Emotions

Emotions are the foundation of the spirit. A person who does not know how to cry will never know how to laugh.

How can a person who judges his own emotions, labeling them as unjust and opportune, be able to consciously recognize his own dreams?

Only someone who unconditionally respects what he feels will be able to recognize when his emotions are telling him that it may be time to adjust the direction he is going in.

You ask me:

What is my mission?

What commitment did I make to heaven before incarnating?

Am I fulfilling this mission?

And then you try to elevate yourself so that you can have access to this information.

There is something that I want you to know.

You can elevate yourself, you can come up here, but it won't get you very far. Unless your emotions are flowing freely through your energetic system, nothing meaningful will ever happen in your life.

Your emotions are the top priority.

A person who feels something but refuses to show what he is feeling, preferring to keep it locked inside and covered up, wishing that it had never emerged and hoping that it will disappear forever so as not to bother him again, so as not to have to make him recall that there are sorrows he never cried over, losses he never mourned . . .

This person deeply wishes that life were a bed of roses without thorns.

This person has failed to understand anything.

He has not understood that everything has two sides to it, that opposites are part of our reality, and that those who do not go through each and every one of their sorrows will find it extremely difficult to experience any joy.

Those who never feel emotional have let go of their sense of feeling, and without feelings nothing has meaning. And life is made of meanings.

It is not all about work, money, and matter.

Those who are able to understand the meaning of things live better lives.

They know what they are doing there.

They know why things happen and how to learn from them.

They know the reason for each loss suffered and how to avoid further loss.

They are able to love everything they do and everyone they interact with. They are aware that it takes only a minute to be awakened and that minute is magical and should not be wasted.

Those who feel, dream.

Those who dream, live.

Those who live, learn.

Those who learn, evolve.

Those who evolve take less time to become closer to me.

JESUS

64

Meaning

Imagine a life without meaning. An empty existence, a life completely devoid of spirituality.

A life without meaning opens the door to a number of confusing and hostile situations.

Not to give meaning to life is to lose yourself in a never-ending web of illusions.

What does it mean to give meaning to life?

It means to fill your life with synonyms for freedom, fraternity, and hope.

It is to know that man's inner self is the most sacred, strangest, addictive, and magical of places.

It is to understand that all of man's wisdom lies within his heart.

To understand the meaning of life and life itself is something that only few are able to do, those who have opened up their hearts and understand the changes that elevation brings.

Only once you have understood this will you fully understand that in the moment of ascension there are and will be downward phases. That in the moment of connection you may be faced with doubts and in the moment of being who you really are you may have moments of hesitation.

But these moments will not jeopardize your journey, they will not prevent things moving forward; the course has been determined, and it is irreversible.

In reality there is only one difference between men and animals.

They say that unlike animals, man is afraid of dying. But animals are also afraid; otherwise they would not run from their predators.

They say that animals do not have a conscience, but if you look closely, you will see that there are many humans who have less sense of what is right and wrong than many animals.

When it comes down to it, the real difference between men and animals is man's intrinsic ability to give meaning to his existence.

And this is possible only if he understands that a life without meaning serves no real purpose.

JESUS

65

Sin

One of the most disgraceful and deplorable characteristics found among religions in general is their tendency to present their followers with ill-founded "truths."

Sin, or whatever name the various religions use to instill prohibition, is a clear example of what I am talking about.

Follow my line of thought: Man is born without knowing that there is continuity.

He does not remember the life he has already lived, he does not recall what he agreed to up here, and he does not recall that there is a future life.

Naturally, when society tells him that there is nothing beyond this life, he has no problem believing this.

The fact that your society removes the notion of eternity from human consciousness is a very serious problem.

Man begins to focus his attention on this life and on this life alone.

As he is not aware that his suffering is a consequence of what he has done and that his past actions will have cosmic consequences.

He focuses on this life, where he is intent on being a winner even if it means stepping on a great number of things—and people—to achieve this.

Consequently, his ego begins to come up with a list of evil doings, which will make his life so much easier once he has carried them out.

And this is where religions enter into the picture—in reality they entered into the picture when they began denying the existence of past and future lives—but now is when they actually begin to gain strength.

They divulge a few sins. They let it be known that those who do not sin will reach salvation.

"Is that it?" asks the being.

Is that all I have to do to reach salvation?

Can I do whatever else I desire?

And since no list of sins has the capacity to explain the law of karma—that is to say, everything you do has consequences in this lifetime or another lifetime—these beings remain at the mercy of this omission in their list of sins.

You must not kill, you must not steal, but you may torture, trample on, and humiliate.

You must not overeat, for this is gluttony, but you may eat additives and preservatives, and you may modify the DNA in food elements.

You may not covet your neighbor's wife, but you can repress your feelings of passion and become emotionally blocked because you have inhibited your emotions.

Clearly, the list of what each of you may or may not do should be focused entirely on your own conscience. It should be at the very heart of who you are as a person.

JESUS

66

Fear of Making Mistakes

When we believe we are doing the right thing, when we want things to work out, we often become obsessed with the need for everything to run smoothly.

This obsession, this compulsive need for continual success, distorts our perception of reality.

The problem lies in our fear of making mistakes. Our constant search for success is the driving force behind the tasks we carry out. This one-sided approach to success is nothing more than a demonstration of our fear, dread, and deep-rooted rejection of making mistakes.

To err is human. To err is essential. Making mistakes is what makes us grow and move forward.

Observe how our mistakes are immediately followed by an inner crisis.

Frustration, sadness and sorrow are keywords here.

My suggestion: Take advantage of your sadness, not rage or guilt but the feeling of helplessness. Take advantage of having attracted the mistake and the consequences that come with it.

Of not having known or not having been able to avoid it.

Sometimes it is others who cause us to make mistakes, although this is also part of the plan.

Use this sadness to your own advantage. Cry. Allow yourself to grieve until there is nothing left to cry over.

Moments of pain. Hours of pain. Sometimes even days of pain.

But this pain will end. When it ends, it is because you have connected with your divine fountain of light, which is at the very core of man—his true "self," where all the answers lie.

Only then will you be ready to start over, to change, and to progress.

Anything you do from now on, you will do with your whole, profound, and sacred being.

Anything you do from now on will make complete sense as you seek to evolve.

Anything you do from now on will be so completely individual, original, and authentic that it will naturally bring innovation and a new light into the world.

As you can see, it was the mistake, the crisis, the experience of pain and subsequent action that influenced this progress, this connection with the evolutionary force. Even if a person finds it difficult to follow a spiritual process through meditation, he may follow it through connecting correctly to his emotions.

Clearly, mistakes are not only useful but acceptable. Mistakes are legitimate and sometimes even desirable.

The people who go through life rationalizing, pondering over things, and trying to avoid making mistakes never take action or simply act in accordance with what is already established, which means the world never advances.

So I am warning you, be careful about making judgments.

When someone does, says, or thinks about things that seem improbable, original, or out of line with current universal thought, before labeling them, before judging them, think about whether this person isn't already deeply connected to his most inner self, to his sacred self, and maybe even to the future of humanity.

JESUS

67

Connection

Meditation and spiritual cleansing are the two most important things that exist.

A person who is disconnected and has density is a person who lacks an inner life, someone who has no life of his own.

Someone who is always focused on others, worried about what others will think or say.

Someone who needs to please others in order to be accepted.

Someone who needs the approval of others in order to be who he is.

A person who is disconnected and has density will never discover his essence, the original source of his life there on earth, the vessel that transports spiritual information, his mission, and his path in life.

A person without a spiritual life is a machine, a robot, a being that is always subservient to others—and you know that the ego is always ready to serve someone.

It is time to free yourself, to cut the chains, to stop paying so much attention to the ego, to connect, and to ascend. It is time to find a life of fulfillment in the midst of density.

A person who is disconnected is an unhappy person.

That is not how you wish to be, is it?

JESUS

68
Learning to Be

When we stop focusing on work, family, friends, material possessions, the person I wanted to be but never was, and the person that I strive to be . . .

When we remove all these focal points from our life, what is left?

If today you were to stop caring for others, whether they are relatives, friends, or those in positions of power, where would your consciousness go? Where would your convictions lie?

If you had nothing that worried you, no money, goals, or objectives, what would be left?

Your inner light would be left.

Your essence would be left, your deepest vibration.

This vibration that comes from the self would be stronger or weaker depending on the number of times you stripped yourself of everything and how often you had sought it out.

The strength of this vibration would be determined by how often you were distracted and by the number of things—often of no importance whatsoever—you found to occupy yourself with.

This vibration is standing by to save your life and to make sure you fulfill your purpose here.

This vibration needs to be cherished, fed, and trained, so that it can shine clearly and steadily and consolidate this incarnation.

If the things you do do not make your light shine, they will neither move forward nor be resolved.

First and foremost, before others, before the great love of your life, before your children and your parents, before your friends and your co-workers, before everything you need to do, even before survival, there is your light. That is where "you" are.

The rest will then appear under the sign of abundance, embracing everything slowly and passionately.

Learn how to make your light shine.

Learn how to do this, and you will be initiated.

JESUS

69
Control

If you were a grain of sand, where would the wind take you?

If you were a grain of sand, where would the wind have you stop?

What would the wind have you experience?

Life has its own movement.

Grains of sand allow themselves to be swept away by the wind because they have no will of their own.

They do not pass judgment. They do not think that this is either good or bad.

They show no desire to go or stay.

They go where the wind takes them.

If you were a grain of sand, you would be so light and accessible that you would accept the direction offered to you, encounter new places, and take on new experiences.

You would have the opportunity to experience new things again.

And your life would be infinitely richer because you would travel and be free, and you would not think that your life was awful or boring.

You would not always be thinking that nothing works out for you.

You would not always be thinking that others are out to harm you.

You would be more concerned about losing density and becoming light so that you would be able to follow the direction of the wind, each time further away and higher up.

If you were a grain of sand, you would be light, intuitive, mobile, and authentic.

And life would not be such a burden.

And things would be easier.

And everything would be in its place.

JESUS

70

Attraction

You are entirely responsible for everything that you attract.

You attract everything that happens to you.

Although it may sound strange, you attract only what you have inside you.

Hence, you will attract violence only if you have violence inside you. You will attract love only if you have love inside you.

Instead of trying to avoid negative things happening to you . . . rather than complaining that only bad things happen to you . . .

Look at things as if they were a mirror image of your inner self.

And express your gratitude.

Thank those who caused you pain for showing you what part of yourself you need to work on.

And work on it.

Show your gratitude and work.

This is the process.

If you attract a violent situation, recognize that this situation is simply a reflection of your inner violence.

Be aware of this, and enter into contact with your inner violence.

Look back on a violent situation that you once experienced and cry, shout, kick out, go through it all, and remove the negative energy inside your heart.

Remove this density, and open up your heart so that I may enter.

And this way, you will be able to cleanse each new situation or event as it arises, always thanking and cleansing.

One day, you will wake up to a realm of love in your heart, and you will know that I am there.

JESUS

71
Relationships

It is very hard to talk about relationships, especially relationships in which people are unable to be themselves. People prefer to live according to others' expectations of them just because it seems easier than trying to be who they really are.

It is when people try to act in accordance with other people's wishes that the soul begins to wane; it becomes disillusioned and sad at not being able to reach full maturity, which is what every soul yearns for.

Each incarnation is an opportunity for the soul to manifest itself.

When those you form relationships with suggest that you stop being yourself and you accept, when your relationships, whether they be with husband, wife, parents, or children or of a professional nature, suggest you forfeit your soul, that which you came to earth to be, in favor of trivial wishes and mental manipulation, it is because the person or persons who share your life do not "see" you. They cannot see your soul.

This happens either because they do not really know you or, worse, because you, too, are unable to see yourself for who you are and end up accepting the situation.

It is not their fault, it is not your fault, there is no blame, only responsibility, and it is you that must take on the responsibility of not abandoning your soul along the way.

Your soul is your light.

Your soul is your life.

And it is up to you to direct these relationships, to set up boundaries, to learn to say, "No, I can't, I don't have to." It is up to you to learn to internalize, to look within yourself, to find your own logic, to discover your own options and opinions, and to make your own choices.

Learn how to be and how to share who you are with others.

It is essential that you respect others and the choices they make, right down to the last tiny detail. Only then will you be in contact with that great hidden force. And when you get to know it well, you will get used to calling it your light.

JESUS

72

My Love

Give them my love.

That is all. Give them my love.

Give them the love that you receive from me.

Do whatever you need to do so that my love reigns in your heart.

Do your best to remove density and the negative and destructive memories and emotions that exist.

Try to avoid having rage, hate, envy, and bitterness in your emotional system.

Reach into your pain as much as you need to, deactivate your memory and then ascend. When you arrive here, make sure that you are light, fresh, and crystalline, so that my love can be blessed, so that my love can embrace the world through your vibrations.

And when you are out on the streets, when you talk to people, when you are where you need to be in your daily life, the enormous amount of love that I feel for humanity will burst forth from you and invade the whole planet.

And you will know that it is I.

You will know that it is I who has invaded the streets and people's souls.

And everything will become clearer.

And everything will become cleaner.

And everything will take on the vibrations of heaven, because this is the only way man has of returning home.

JESUS

73
Peace

There is a peace that can be reached only when we make the right decisions.

Decisions that are right for you, of course.

Most people make decisions based on the idea that "it has to be done," "there is no other choice," "I really have to do this."

These are decisions forced on us by our mind, by a controlling and sinister ego that keeps itself hidden from the soul because it is fearful of the soul's strength.

I will say it once again: when our original energy is respected in the decision-making process, these decisions have enormous strength. This happens because everything falls into place once a person shows self-respect and is aware that what may be good for him may not necessarily be good for others.

Every time you make a decision, do as follows: close your eyes, even if it is just for a second, and feel your heart. More important, get in touch with your intuition. The heart sometimes suffers from the decisions that are made based on our intuition. Allow yourself to feel it.

Is there peace? Is there energetic coherence? Is there an ancient feeling that "everything is in its place"?

If the answer is yes, it is right. Your decision is correct.

If not, you know what you have to do.

JESUS

74

Intuition

Do you know how penguins know it is time to migrate?

When they are walking and the ice beneath their feet starts to break.

They are walking along as usual, and they feel the ice begin to crack.

This incident, this minuscule and extraordinary incident, affects the life of millions of penguins, which, from that moment forward, know the time has come. It is time to depart to even less hospitable places, so that they may proceed with their yearly venture of pro-creating.

It has been like this for millions of years. The ice cracks, and they depart only to return much later with their young, one more to add to their species. It has been like this for millions of years.

And it will continue to be so.

Man has intuitive skills. He can feel when it is time for things to happen even before the ice breaks beneath his feet. Even before things happen, human beings are able to feel that the time has arrived.

And it has been like this for millions of years.

Man, however, makes judgments. He chooses to believe that he cannot do things or, even if he can, that intuition is not a good thing.

So he covers things up. And so he becomes blocked.

Man blocks his most magnanimous aptitude, his ability to walk before time and ensure that everything happens as it is meant to happen, simply because this is what he has perceived.

Man has a tendency to block out not only this skill but almost every other skill that he possesses.

"I can't do it."

"I don't deserve it."

"This is too good for me."

These are expressions that, repeated a million times, are likely to become true.

Believe in your intuition. It is powerful and life-changing.

You may not believe in anything else, but at least believe in your intuition.

It may not change the world, but it will probably change your world.

And that in itself is already more than enough.

JESUS

75

Effort

You cannot do things by force.

Every time you try too hard, you shut down the channel with heaven.

Exertion is the opposite of levity. Levity is a product of heaven.

Exertion is dense; levity is made of light.

Whenever you require too much effort, it means that things are not running smoothly and additional resources are needed.

And why are additional resources required?

Because things are not following their natural order, which should be both magical and calm, which in turn means they are simply not meant to happen.

The water runs smoothly and clearly down the waterfall, and as it falls, it continues to flow and to sing.

Life is the same.

If you realize that the things that require too much effort are not meant to be . . .

If you understand that life has an order that you must respect . . .

You will begin to exert yourself less and enjoy things more.

And your life, from one moment to the next, will become a life you enjoy living.

JESUS

76

Enemies

When a person upsets you, it is natural to think badly of him. You start to think that he could have done things differently; he could have reacted more calmly . . .

All these thoughts are part of the judgment process.

You wanted this person to say or do things your way.

You wanted him to convince you.

You wanted him to make you feel comfortable.

However, the Universe does not work this way.

The magnet that lies within your heart, that powerful energetic sensor that attracts what is destined for you in so many different ways, will naturally attract the person or thing that will go on to help you experience the emotions you need to face.

But I am sure that you already know this.

What you may not know is that the main emotion that crops up in all the situations you attract is the same emotion you experienced in other lifetimes and throughout your childhood.

What do I mean by this?

That the person or situation you are facing at this moment holds the key to your innermost secret. He or it holds the key to your karma.

If you accept that this person or situation is part of your life, that you attracted him or it so that you could release this emotion, and that this is your top priority . . .

If you accept that this person is there to help you with this . . .

That he is there to help you release your density, regardless of the outcome . . .

You will realize that this person must be your soul companion, a being you once shared wonderful secrets with up in the clouds, before you incarnated.

He must be a friend from the soul.

If you stop judging him and blaming him for how he has made you feel . . .

If you stop judging him and instead acknowledge that he is here to help you . . .

You will immediately stop focusing on him and what he makes you go through and start focusing on your heart, which is having difficulty deciding whether to process this huge emotion or block it out forever.

When the mind rules the heart, this sort of thing often happens.

And if you focus on yourself, on your heart, you will experience enormous pain, the pain that you have been continuously running from.

But once the pain has gone—because it always disappears—your life will take on a new dimension.

Every time you overcome an emotional blockage in density, you will move toward the light.

The next time you look at the person who hurt you, you will know that it was a learning experience.

And you will know how to respond.

And you will be grateful for the lesson you have learned.

JESUS

77
Wanting

Your feet were made for walking
   —Stop trying to walk;
   Your legs were made to support your body
   —Stop trying to support your body;
   Your back was made to sustain the world
   —Stop trying to sustain the world;
   Your frame was made to hold you up
   —Stop trying to hold yourself up;
   Your stomach was made to contain food
   —Stop trying to contain your food;
Food was made to give your body energy
   —Stop trying to give your body energy;
   Your neck was made to support your head
   —Stop trying to support your head;
   Your brain was made to sustain your ego
   —Stop trying to sustain your ego;
The ego was made to keep control
   —Stop trying to keep control;
Control was made to shift fear
   —Stop trying to shift fear;
Fear was created to incite you to want things
   —Stop inciting this need for things
Wanting was made so that you could run from pain
   —Stop trying to run from your pain.

JESUS

78

The Underworld

Abundance means to fill the underworld with light.

Heaven is not the only place where you find light.

It is not enough just to come up here.

You have to visit your own underworld; you have to keep revisiting it until the light begins to seep through.

The truth is that the more you visit your personal underworld, the more you revisit this dense stage of humanity, and the more you get in touch with the underwater monster that is within each of us, the more the earth will begin to elevate as one.

The more you visit the darkness as a way of freeing yourself from it, of letting it go unconditionally, the greater will be the light that reaches you.

In ascension . . .

There is no calling that goes unanswered;

There is no error that goes unpardoned;

There is no excess that goes uncompensated;

There is no karma that does not have courage;

There is no dharma that does not have light;

There is no step without a road;

There is no land that does not lie vacant.

JESUS

79

The Path

When people ask heaven questions, they tend to believe that they will always receive positive answers.

They are not ready to face loss. They are not ready to be misled.

They are not ready to face reality.

Just because they have received a sign or been told which path to follow by their higher self, they now believe that they will never again encounter obstacles or crossroads.

Nothing could be further from the truth.

When heaven points out a path, it may well be the best path to go down, it may well coincide with your original energy, it may well be the path to evolution. It may be all these things.

However, if you have to experience something but are not ready for the experience, you will end up facing loss on the path to light.

Our path is but one. It is the most truthful, most original, and most accurate. Nevertheless, it is still just a path. And as such, it has bends, obstacles, and stones.

Do not forget: Everything in matter has two sides. Good and evil, in equal amounts.

But this path has an advantage over all the rest.

It is yours.

As long as you do not abandon your path, everything that your soul experiences throughout this journey, everything that you need to experience will enhance your evolution.

This is the advantage it has. I never said that living was easy. But no opposing path can help you evolve. Any path that does not have your original energy will make things even harder for you.

Therefore, choose your path, the path that is yours, the one that has your color and texture. Stay on that path. And don't forget, never stop feeling. If you stop feeling, your energy will automatically be removed.

And regardless of the tight spots you get into, regardless of the deviations and confusion, this path has something advantageous, something that no other will ever have.

This path will lead you to me.

JESUS

80
Simplicity

When was the last time you picked a wildflower and just sat looking at it?

Just sat there, looking at a simple flower?

How long has it been since you last did this?

Instead of living in the past and feeling bitter over the wrong choices you have made and the things people have supposedly done to you . . .

Instead of living in the future and fantasizing about what you are going to do and be, simply pick a flower and sit there looking at it.

Put aside thoughts of the past and future, put aside your plans, ambitions, sorrows, and resentment.

Just remain where you are, gazing at this simple flower.

Put aside all emotional burdens, dilemmas, projections, and deferments.

Put all thoughts aside.

Just stay as you are, gazing at this flower.

How long has it been?

This is the secret to life: finding things that make time stop or finding the time to make things stop, so that you may just observe them.

So that you may simply remain where you are.

So that you may simply be who you are.

JESUS

81

The Inner Journey

Human beings. All my actions are focused on human beings.

Every word, every expression.

It is they whom I talk about, it is they I am concerned about, and it is they I dedicate everything to.

Human beings. All my actions are focused on human beings.

Each of my words is inspired by man's suffering and his inability to free himself from his pain.

In his search for happiness, man has crossed boundaries, built monuments, sailed through unknown seas, reached the moon, wandered through the stars, and built devices to observe the galaxies.

Yet in his search for happiness, man has always searched outside himself.

Happiness is the capacity man has to look within himself and to face his demons head-on. It is not about avoiding them but about revealing and confronting them.

We have yet to build a ship that can make the journey to the depths of our inner self.

Would you like me to take you?

JESUS

82

Inversion

Every concept has been altered.

The whole of humanity has stopped making an effort, causing a rise in densities.

The earth no longer bows down to heaven.

Everything has been inverted.

There is nothing of value. There is no future.

It is time to guide people's efforts in another direction, to repair divisions.

To reverse what has been done. To rectify what is behind this error.

To go to the opposite. To redefine.

JESUS

83

Energetic Connections

Everything you do has repercussions. All your actions have consequences.

No matter how innocent your actions are, the consequences will not take long in coming.

No matter how small the deflection, it is always necessary to go back and harmonize things.

Think about this:

The Universe is energetically perfect. At this precise moment, everything is as it should be—in order to accomplish the mission it was destined for.

When man tampers with the natural order of things, he is disharmonizing that which cannot be disharmonized.

What do I mean by this? I mean that whether you like it or not, whatever is moved needs to be put back in its rightful place.

It is inevitable.

So whenever you harm someone, no matter how small the act, think about the fact that sooner or later you will experience what this person has experienced, so that the axle of emotions—hurt/be hurt, can be harmonized.

Whether you are teasing or mocking someone, remember that sooner or later you too will find yourself being mocked.

Nature never fails.

So take a close look at the energetic connections that tie you to the people you have harmed or to the unpleasant things you have provoked. If you can salvage things, then do so.

Try to harmonize things before life sends you an unpleasant situation as a way of reharmonizing.

If you are not able to salvage things, try to spread love and light around you, so that the energy that surrounds you recognizes that you have changed and spares you the consequences of your former acts.

JESUS

84

The Ego

I have always told you that the ego is the worst of all evils. It is the ego that teaches you to want and to fight for things that energetically are not right for you.

It is the ego that barks out and cancels the orders inside your brain. It is the ego that makes you vibrate through restriction and through fear.

It is also the ego that surrounds you in a bubble of illusion, so that you can truly believe in whatever you wish to believe:

That you will be happy and that you should pay no attention to the growing dissatisfaction you feel in your heart.

That on the day you receive new clothes, a computer, a new car, a house, that is to say, everything you really deserve, you will achieve happiness.

And when you grow weary of waiting, the ego convinces you not to give up; it convinces you that you are almost there . . .

"Work hard just a little while longer, ignore what you are feeling just a little while longer, keep fighting just a little while longer," it tells you.

But that "little while longer" never ends.

Yet the ego keeps on insisting that resistance and struggle are the only way forward. It does not allow you to see that resistance and struggle take you nowhere or, worse yet, that they continue to take you energetically down the wrong path.

The road ahead is not one of resistance and struggle.

You should be traveling in the opposite direction.

Acceptance and fruition are the road you should follow.

Accept the situation you are in, and begin to allow the buoy to float so that the current can lead you to safe harbors.

And you may then move toward that which awaits you in this incarnation.

JESUS

85

Choice

You can always choose. You can choose to go where your Higher Self and I suggest—to a place where you will be protected and saved—or to go to the place where you want to be, but that affords you no protection. I am not going to change the energy of places just so that you can be okay.

People need to understand that the Universe doesn't change simply to please them. Either you discover where the Universe is headed and you follow it, or you will end up having traumatic experiences.

To go where the Universe is headed is an ecological goal.

An ecological goal may mean that what you desire is in harmony with the Universe, either because you just happened to be in agreement or because you have connected, received, and accepted our suggestion and then proceeded in accordance with it.

By doing this you will be protected. You will be protected because what you are doing is in harmony with your original energy. To live solely and exclusively in the function of your original energy is the greatest wisdom that can exist there on earth. It would mean no more loss and no more traumas.

However, it is also good for you to experience the opposite of this, to see things that you never imagined, and to go through intense emotional traumas. One can also evolve through conflict.

All the same, you could have evolved without all this suffering.

All you had to do was listen to me.

JESUS

86

Rituals

Sometimes energy is very dense and rituals are extremely ancient. So many rituals have been performed for the ego's benefit, in keeping with people's wishes.

People wanted rain, they performed rituals. They wanted to harm someone, they performed rituals. They were about to go to war, they performed rituals. Everything was about the survival of the lower spirit. Ancient practices made no attempt at evolution. All that existed was an instinct for survival.

Lesser spirits would approach. As it was easy to provide human beings with what they wanted, these spirits would trade with them. They would give them the results they desired, such as rain, victory, or someone else's downfall. In exchange, they would stay on, taking over the spiritual world close to matter and setting down roots.

Now they dominate the ether close to the earth.

Today, there are places and people that are completely drained because they carry the energy of those who continuously evoked the spirits.

Carried out entirely for self-benefit.

Completely contrary to evolution.

JESUS

87

Essence

Your essence is always waiting for you.

It is always waiting for you to stop looking to others.

It is also always waiting for you to stop looking to me.

It is there, waiting for you, so that it can be.

So that it can give you the strength to vibrate through your original energy.

Your essence is a being of light confined within your physical body.

It wishes to be free, it wants to fly, it wants much more than the restrictive life you are willing to give it.

It would like its light, its enormous light, to embrace the world and to enchant everyone with its powerful convictions.

But for this to happen, you have to recognize it.

For this to happen, you have to understand and embrace it.

You have to recognize it and go after it.

You have to understand that your essence is you, in your purest form, in your most original state. You have to feel that this essence is you at the time you were up here with us, sharing the boundless space that is heaven.

Only when you have understood how magnificent your own essence is, only when you have understood how sacred and unique this energy is, will you be able to understand the true being of light that you are and what you came down to earth to do.

JESUS

88

Responsibility

You are not responsible for anyone.

There is nothing in this world that can force you to step out of your center.

There is nothing in this world that can force you to put other people first.

Do you know why there are so many people who cannot meditate?

Because when they close their eyes and look into their heart, they see so many other people, so many other obligations, their heart is so burdened . . .

They end up feeling anguished and stop meditating. What they should do is remove the burden of responsibility they feel in their heart. They need to understand that they are not responsible for others.

Everyone comes down to earth to fulfill a purpose. However, if someone takes your place, you are prevented from cleansing your karma.

Those who take responsibility for others or feel guilty for not looking after them feel like this because they have not yet realized how much they are harming them.

They are not allowing them to take responsibility for cleansing their own karma.

They are removing the responsibility they have for the choices they make.

They are removing their initiative.

They are removing their essence.

And lastly, they are removing their light.

When you take responsibility for other people, you are running away from yourself, you are running away from essence, but, most important, you are running away from your own light.

Now do you understand?

JESUS

89

Lies

Why do people lie to each other?

Why do people lie to themselves?

Simply because it is easier than facing reality.

Confronting a person with something he does not want to accept can be very awkward. How can you go about this?

Let's address one thing at a time.

Lying to yourself. This is the worst lie of all, the one that diminishes a person. The person who does this is unable to accept himself. Not only does he refuse to accept his limitations and shortcomings, but he does not accept that he is different from others. Above all, he refuses to accept that he is not meant to be like others nor as others expect him to be.

This being is always in conflict with himself. He will never be happy. He creates an illusion and believes it will bring him greater comfort, without the slightest concern as to what it may do to his original energy.

Then there are those who lie to others.

These beings are simply cowards. I am not saying that you have to share every single part of your life with others. If you don't wish to tell people something, don't. Every human being should create an air of mystery around himself. There is no harm in this.

But lying, pretending that something is true when it is not, is something else altogether.

You can simply say that you do not want to comment on the situation or that you do not feel like talking.

But never lie.

Do not forget that all your actions have consequences. And from the moment a lie becomes an energetic manipulation of the truth, it will always bring manipulative consequences.

I doubt very much you will like the outcome.

JESUS

90
Ascension

Inner conflict is the key to the wheel of incarnations.

A being descends and incarnates because he is tied up on the wheel of incarnations. He is bound to this wheel through conflict.

Unless he is able to resolve his inner conflict, until he is able to find peace with his conflicting opposites, he will never be able to ascend, and, as a result, he will never step out of the wheel of incarnations.

To let go of conflict is to understand that the world is made up of opposites.

To let go of conflict is to believe, as hard as this may seem, that these opposites can coexist.

On the day you believe that extreme opposites may coexist . . .

On the day you realize that you may have your own opinions yet someone else may see the world differently and have his own opinions . . .

On the day you stop believing that your opinions are right and those of others wrong and you begin to understand they are simply two opinions—just two opinions, two different ways of looking at life, just two opposites on the same axis. Neither one is better than the other, for there is more than enough space for two different perspectives on life; in fact, there is room for many more. And they are all correct. They are all viable. And they are all possible . . .

On the day you allow yourself to feel two opposing emotions within your heart, allow them to simply coexist, without judgment, without feeling that one is better than the other . . .

On the day you are able to vibrate in this frequency that is so elevated and seems so unattainable to human beings . . .

On that day, conflict will be abolished.

And you will be ready to ascend. You will be ready to step out of the wheel of incarnations, to ascend up here and feel another type of energy.

On ascending up here, you can then continue your evolution in new horizons.

JESUS

91
Perfection

Perfection does not exist. Since it is not an objective, it cannot be an end in itself.

You should want only to reach a place that is inviting, comfortable, and light.

Human beings are not supposed to want to go a place that is disharmonized and unbalanced.

For this is perfection. It is a state of demand, stress, anguish, and depression.

It is a place where people hold too many expectations, yet it is also an unknown place. Since it does not exist, no one has ever been there, other than for a few brief moments.

The problem is that people do not take this into consideration.

They want to be perfect.

They struggle to be perfect. They judge everything that is imperfect and in doing so take away its value.

Man fails to understand that:

Heaven is perfect.

The Universe is perfect.

Heaven shelters beings of light.

The world shelters men—imperfect beings in search of evolution. And how are they going to evolve?

By entering into contact with the world's imperfection so that, and because of, their struggle with this imperfection, they may evolve and move forward.

Now imagine that human beings were perfect. There would be no conflict, and seeing that it is through conflict that we evolve, there would be no evolution.

Everything would be perfect, and we would never have gone through this experience on earth.

And now what do we need to do?

We need to make peace with our own imperfections. Accept that we are not perfect, nor do we have to be. What we should do, instead, is our best, in a more responsible way.

That is all.

And just by your doing this, I, from up here, will be very happy.

JESUS

92

For Whose Sake?

For whose sake?

Yes, this is my question. You are born, grow up, go to school, choose a career, choose partners, date, marry, have children, and work. You put up with pressure from your parents, your partner, your children, and your boss, as well as money and society.

This is my question:

For whose sake do you do a job you do not enjoy, and for whose sake do you put up with overbearing parents?

For whose sake do you put up with the demands of a partner who fails to accept you for who you are?

For whose sake do you put up with the demands your children place on you as a parent?

For whose sake?

For whose sake do you put up with the ups and downs of a career that is taking you nowhere?

For whose sake do you stop traveling, stop doing the things that reenergize your soul?

For whose sake do you allow yourself to get stuck in an insignificant and unproductive life, which is going nowhere and offers you no perspective or satisfaction?

For whose sake?

For whose sake did you lock away your dreams in a drawer and avidly pursue that sense of security that you continue to fall short of?

For whose sake did you forfeit a bright and radiant future, the fruit of your essence's energy?

For whose sake did you reduce your essence, ignore your soul, and crystallize your energy?

This is all I ask.

For whose sake?

JESUS

93
Stopping

You attract everything that takes place. Each and every event, each and every moment in time. Everything that happens is caused by the energy you emanate.

Sometimes you are aware of it, other times you are not, but every manner, thought, action, and reaction, and each and every moment you go through is filled with this energy.

And this energy comes out through your pores, the chakras, your eyes.

Every one of your intentions has an energy of its own. Every contained moment emanates force.

Everything that happens in your life, right down to the tiniest detail, is simply a response to that individual and unique energy you are sending out into the Universe.

If one day, you stopped everything—stopped doing, stopped reacting, thinking, rationalizing, passing judgment, if one day, you stopped everything in your life . . .

If you stopped everything and just remained quiet, feeling things, on that day, you would no longer experience the things that have been troubling you over the last few years. All that would remain on the day you consciously stop emanating energy are the events that respond to your unconscious energy.

This unconscious energy, which you emanate when you are not doing anything, is the purest memory of past lives. This energy produces only events that you need to experience in order to liberate yourself from the emotion they provoke in you.

And afterward?

What would happen once you stopped emanating conscious energy and cleansed this unconscious energy?

There would be no more energy left to emanate and therefore no events resulting from this energy.

It is here, at this exact point in time, that you would really begin living your life.

Only at this point would you be free of your instinctive and unconscious emotions and have the peace of mind to make your own choices.

To sum up:

Your conscious actions are determined by energy from your unconscious memory.

The energy from this memory is emanated as a way of attracting new events that bring about the emotions you need to experience.

Only when you stop this movement of conscious actions will you be able to access your subconscious energy and cleanse your memories. On cleansing these memories, you will free yourself from this unconscious, instinctive energy.

Given that you have changed your energy, when you start to move forward again, you will be confronted with different consequences. These consequences will be much more real, clear, cleansed, and light.

These are the dynamics of attraction. This is what you need to understand if you wish to change your life.

JESUS

94

Victimization

A child cries to call attention to himself. This is something we all agree on. It is self-evident.

The child cries because he is afraid of pain, of what hurts him, of the tightness in his chest.

The child cries, and his crying captures everyone's attention.

The child is a victim.

He believes someone else is to blame for his discomfort and waits for someone to come along and alleviate it.

It always comes down to others.

The child falls, hits his arm against the table, but does not see himself as responsible. It is the table's fault.

And so he goes on crying, throwing tantrums, waiting for someone to fuss over him and to take away any and every responsibility he may hold while showering him with love and affection.

The child receives love and affection when he cries. He receives comfort. He receives protection.

But this child grows up. And strangely enough, he does not change his way of thinking. As an adult he continues to complain and whine about others, the "bad guys," those who have supposedly hurt him.

This grown-up child craves attention.

He does not take responsibility for his actions. He never takes responsibility for anything that happens to him.

He does not want to acknowledge that people attract only what is already in their heart.

Those who are violent attract violence.

"Bad guys" do not exist. Everyone and everything, without exception, is attracted by your energy. They are not bad. They are vehicles that heaven uses as a way of helping you experience the things you need to experience.

Yet instead of acknowledging this once and for all, instead of changing your energy and taking responsibility for what you attract, even if it is only so that you may cleanse your heart of that frequency and stop attracting such events, you blame others, complain about your bad luck, and play the victim.

Are you looking for attention?

This child is now grown up and needs to change his attitude; he needs to be more mature and take control of the life he has chosen on this journey.

Are you looking for attention?

Change, look within, meditate, and find your essence, your true inner self. Come up here to find my unconditional love, and you will receive all the attention that exists in this lifetime.

JESUS

95

Entering into Others

Reach inside each person.

Step deep inside.

Place your conscience inside their heart.

Place your mind inside their eyes.

What do they see?

What does each of them see in this lifetime, this world? How do they see you?

If the person is a friend of yours, see things through his or her eyes.

Stay there for a while, in meditation.

Do not be afraid to get involved.

Do not be afraid to move away from the position you hold, your hard and insensitive stance. Go there and see things through his eyes. See things as he sees them.

What do such people desire?

How could they live better lives?

I did not say more comfortable lives. Put comfort aside. I said live better, with more quality and greater tranquillity.

With more soul.

How can you get their souls to come out and rejoice in their existence?

You may know how.

Just observe, from down there, how the world functions when things are at their best.

JESUS

96

Loving Others

Love others. Love each and every person. Love his or her soul.

If you do not like someone, if that person has a lot of faults, I dare you to discover his or her good qualities.

I dare you to discover that person's soul, to recognize that you attracted that soul and that it attracted you, which, more than likely, did not happen by chance.

Whatever it is that you came to do on earth, you came to do it together. Given that there are things you must accomplish, it's best that you do them well, with harmony and sincerity.

Love people's souls, help them to give up their resistance and open the way to acceptance.

Talk, as friends, about your different points of view and make a personal alliance in which you both gain something. In which you can both see yourselves achieving something.

There is no soul that does not desire harmony.

There is no soul that does not desire love.

There truly isn't.

JESUS

97

Feeling Sad

When someone you really care about hurts you . . .

Feel sad.

Get in touch with your pain for the benefit of the souls who are unable to understand one another.

Just feel sad.

If you feel very sad, cry. The tears that flow will be well received.

And show your sadness. Explain how it hurts you and how good it would be if you could work this out.

Invite that soul to open up its heart. Without regret. Without judgment.

Judgment is what normally destroys relationships.

People do not open up their hearts because they judge others.

And because they judge others, they think others judge them.

And they become angry.

And they judge even more, and this vicious circle drastically feeds off itself.

This is the cycle of pain.

After showing someone how much you hurt, ask him to open his heart to you.

To harmonize for you.

To focus within for you.

And you will receive a favor.

And you will always recognize that this person did this for you.

And you will be grateful.

And you will always recognize that people do things for you.

And that you will always receive.

And you will always be grateful.

And they will feel this, and they will continue to do more, and you will thank them even more.

This is the cycle of happiness.

JESUS

98

Dancing

Try to discover what tune people dance to.

The oppressed are oppressed even before they meet their oppressor.

And the oppressor is an oppressor before he attracts the oppressed.

When they attract each other, those on the outside are amazed at how much one person is able to dominate the other.

But it is not quite how it seems. They suit each other perfectly and dance to the same tune. And (as you like to say), it takes two to tango.

No one can dance the tango alone.

You just need to understand each person's logic.

When two people get together, there are always areas in which they differ. Both will have to use freedom of choice and memory to choose a positive area, an area with light to share in this lifetime.

They may actually choose the dense area that unites them and expand it as far as they possibly can.

It is up to them.

If you are able to understand each person's limits, if you can discover the "tune" he dances to, all you have to do is dismantle this fallacy.

When both of them realize that they are part of each other's karmic memory and that they can choose to move away from it, they may choose to step out of it, and they may actually end up gaining awareness and leaving there hand in hand.

JESUS

99

Love and Fear

Which energy makes you move forward?

Love or fear?

In truth, there are only two frequencies that exist down there in matter.

And you need to choose only one.

Either you choose love, or you choose fear.

You choose to vibrate for me, or you choose to vibrate for darkness.

Do you miss anyone? Vibrate through love.

When you miss someone and that longing hurts, even in the midst of this pain, you may vibrate through love.

How?

It is simple.

When you vibrate through negativity, through the longing you feel for that person, when you vibrate through the pain of not having that person, you are vibrating through fear.

Fear of losing that person.

Fear of not having that person.

If you choose to vibrate for me, through the unconditional love that heaven gives you, think only about how much you love that person, even if he is far away.

Feel that love deeply.

And remain there, simply feeling that love.

You will notice your heart filling with light and all your sadness disappearing.

When you are feeling sad, hurt, unhappy, or anxious because of something that has happened . . .

It means you are vibrating through fear. You are afraid of suffering, and so you reject the pain that is part of this experience.

Consequently, you reject the experience. But even here you may choose to vibrate through love. Just think of this experience as a means of getting you to shed a few tears.

And those tears have been waiting a long time to be shed.

This event will provide you with a unique opportunity to cry, to experience a pain that is probably older than you realize.

And as you vibrate through love, you will come to love this new-found awareness that tells you that sad experiences take place as a way of allowing us to mourn our ancient sorrows.

You love being aware.

You love the Universe that brought you this experience.

You love yourself for having understood it.

And last, you love me for having taught you all of this.

JESUS

100
Hearing Me

You are aware of what happened when I was there on earth, spreading my message of peace, brotherhood, love, and solidarity.

There were scandals, there were those who heard my word and accepted me, those who ignored me, even those who cursed me.

There were those who slapped me, washed their hands of me, those who whipped me and those who provoked me.

But there were also those who loved me and those who lost me, and that loss was so painful that it still hurts today.

There are some who have never recovered.

Yet, if you look closely, all this happened in matter.

Everything that happened two thousand years ago took place outside man.

Some men laughed at me, others cried for me.

But no one, not one of them, did anything for themselves.

They listened to my words, but they did not transform them into their own words.

And this is the reason I have returned.

This time around, I want you to convert them into your own words.

I no longer come as a man. I do not come in the form of matter.

No one will ever have to look outside himself or herself in order to see me.

This time around, I come as energy. I come to light up men's hearts.

I want to enter into your heart. I want to enter and, by making you look at me, make you look within yourself.

And you will hear me inside you.

And you will think that my words are yours.

That my thoughts are yours.

And in loving me, you will finally love yourself.

And at that point I will have performed my greatest miracle.

JESUS

101
Powerlessness

You have longed for things since you were a child.

When you were little, you wanted to have lots of friends, you didn't want to go to school, and you didn't want the teachers to hassle you.

As a teenager, you wanted the person you fell in love with to love you back, you wanted to be free, to have your own space, and to have your parents not hassle you too much.

Then, as an adult, you wanted a good job, you wanted money, and to have your boss not hassle you too much.

As life advances, I become more aware of how much you crave things.

You want to be known, you want to be different, you want people to accept you and praise you. And you believe this happens only to people who have power.

Therefore, you want power.

There is something I need to tell you:

Everything you aim for in this lifetime, everything your ego desires, serves to make you feel secure at a subconscious level.

And why do you wish to feel secure? Because you cannot bear to feel insecure. It is too distressing and too painful.

And why do people react so negatively to insecurity? Because they carry memories from past lives.

The person who wishes to have power in this lifetime does so because he or she carries the memory of having had power in another lifetime. And this power made them feel secure. Or they carry a memory of not having had any power at all, which would have made life very difficult.

When someone feels insecure in this lifetime, he immediately remembers, at a subconscious level, the life in which he used power to mask his insecurity. As a result, he pursues power as a way of covering up his insecurity.

I have some bad news.

Since we are speaking of memory, no matter how much power people obtain in this lifetime, they will never be satisfied.

Why?

Because it is that "other" power they pursue, the power they had in that other life.

And their dissatisfaction keeps growing.

And the more they pursue power, the more dissatisfied they feel, because this is not the power they seek.

People come into this lifetime specifically to relinquish that power. They come to let go of that memory. To harmonize. What they had too much of in another lifetime will be harmonized in this lifetime, in the form of restriction.

The more someone pursues power, the more dissatisfied he will feel and the greater the state of powerlessness he will attract.

This is the law of nature.

When people accept all these experiences of powerlessness, regardless of how painful they are, the closer they will become to their essence, the closer they will become to their original energy, and the more secure they will feel.

And the closer they will be to me.

JESUS

102
Soul Mates

Never forget your connections. Every being that crosses your path has a soul that is connected to you in some way, somewhere, within the boundless space of eternity.

Every soul you cross paths with has something to tell you, something to teach you.

When you were up in heaven, in between lives, you decided that whatever it is you needed to learn, you would learn from one other. However, there are some beings whose souls are connected more to your soul than to other souls.

And in this lifetime, there is a being whose soul is connected to yours more than to any other soul.

And it is this being who will be your companion at all times, throughout the good and the bad times.

The connection between your soul and the soul of this very special being exists for one reason only:

To be. For you two to be side by side throughout this journey.

For this reason alone.

Feel this: two souls, side by side, throughout this journey.

That is all. Nothing more.

Exchanging energy and experiences, without ego, without defenses, without obstructions.

Two beings, side by side, sharing one path.

Each soul is who it is.

Each soul is who it is, and it respects the other soul. Nothing more. That is all.

But not all souls are able to reach this level of evolution.

More often than not, these souls continue to have a lot of defenses, a lot of resistance, and a lot of ego.

They are unable to see the way.

They are unable to see the soul they share their journey with.

They are unable to see themselves.

In this state, these souls are unable to evolve. They may be together, but it serves no purpose. There are no emotions. There is no communion. There is no sharing. There are simply two bodies following the same path. That is all.

Let me suggest something.

Begin to look at people as if they were simply souls. Take away their clothes and their bodies. Take away their defenses and resistance. Take away their ego.

You will see a light.

And then do the same to yourself. Remove your body, your defenses, your resistance, and your ego.

And remain in light.

And you will come to realize that conflict, sadness, resentment, and sorrow are not part of the soul.

They are part of matter; they are part of the body, which is fearful.

Eventually, you will even become aware of a soul trapped in a body that did not choose the light.

And the soul is suffering.

When you meet someone, regardless of who he is, do as follows. In your mind, remove his clothes, body, defenses, and resistance and try to feel his soul. You will feel the light from that person's soul.

And you will start to see him in a different light.

You will feel his soul.

You will feel communion.

You will feel both your souls sharing this path.

You will feel their energy.

You will feel me.

JESUS

103

My Voice

Believe that you can be my voice on earth.

You won't be the first, and you certainly will not be the last, but you will be an important voice once you begin to understand the relevance of my words.

You will become my voice not because of what you begin to say but because of what you begin to feel.

Once you begin to feel deeply and are able to emanate my light.

Once you are able to make people feel your energy.

Once you are able to get them to access their own light.

It is not what you say but the energy you put into what you are saying.

It is the light that you put into what you say.

It is the emotion that emanates from your words.

Believe that you can be my voice on earth. Not because of the level of importance this affords you but because of the level of commitment it demands from you. And to be my voice on earth, you will always have to carry my voice inside you.

My voice, my energy, my light, and my inspiration.

You will have to do three things to be my voice on earth: feel, feel, and feel.

The way you feel the light on a sunny day.

The way you feel the pain of a soul that has been betrayed.

The way you feel the immensity of space and time.

Clearly, being human has its limitations.

But practice. Meditate. Access your original energy.

I will be there, waiting for you.

JESUS

104

Protection

To feel protected is to count on God.

To count on us, up here, to help you through each moment of your journey.

Wherever life passes, whatever you go through, count on us.

We, from up here, have the ability to help you, to guide you.

Count on us to guide you along every path you intend to take.

Recognize that everything you touch outside yourself must come from within you. Otherwise, it will be of no use energetically.

Illuminate your way with our light to allow time for your own light to shine.

Come up to heaven, ask questions, entrust us with each issue, each situation.

And really feel the direction of the wind.

For it is the wind that will guide you down there.

Feel how each situation has its own energy and how the magic comes from allowing us to guide you to where the most marvelous transformations may take place.

For you are there to transform.

Ask for protection.

Feel the way and ask for protection.

And understand that, with heaven's blessing, man can reach the end of the world.

JESUS

105
Newness

There is an age-old structure that is weighing on you. It is preventing you from moving forward. It is stopping you from evolving.

That structure is the past.

The person you were in the past, what you felt in the past, but, most of all, how you thought in the past.

The accumulation of concepts, judgments, and feelings of victimization.

All the guilt, fear, and resentment you withstood.

All those burdens that are no longer in keeping with the person you are today but still remain, ready to explode and show how much they weigh on you.

Let go of your past. You are no longer the person you used to be.

You are no longer the person you were five minutes ago.

Everything is changing so fast right now. Why don't you take advantage of this?

Try to let go. With each feeling, with each action and in each situation, invest in the new person you are becoming with a new awareness, new values, a new way of thinking.

With a new essence.

Be who you are today.

It may not be in keeping with your past. It does not matter. We are in the age of change.

And the day will arrive when you will wake up, look in the mirror, and see the enlightened being you have become.

JESUS

106

The Gift of Life

If you consider that nothing, absolutely nothing is yours . . .

If you consider that you have nothing when you come to earth and that you take nothing with you when you leave . . .

If you consider that you are not entitled to anything and that everything you receive is a gift from life . . .

Then you will begin to see life in a different light.

For example:

If you believe something is going to happen to you, yet it does not happen . . .

If you hope that something is going to be resolved in a certain way, yet the outcome is not what you expected . . .

If you want things to work out in a specific way, but they insist on working out differently . . .

If you believe that someone is going to react in a certain way and he reacts differently, or if you wish he had done something he did not do . . .

It is obvious that you will end up feeling disappointed.

You did not expect things to turn out as they did.

But I want to explain something to you.

If there is nothing or no one that belongs to you, how can you wish for things?

What makes you think that you can manipulate things in order to please yourself?

Why would you think that things are going to go your way?

It is life, my friend; it is life that gives you everything. Absolutely everything. Life gives you everything, from the air you breathe to the clothes you wear, the children you have, your friends, your education, your money, job, and relationships.

Have you noticed how many things and people life has already bestowed upon you? Why are you always focused on what you do not have?

Because you wish you had them.

And to want is part of the ego.

You believe you are entitled to a certain amount of things, but for what reason? Who gave them to you?

Who said they were yours?

It was your ego that filled your head with the illusion that you have a right to everything.

Let me suggest something.

Forget everything. Let everything go and start from zero.

Imagine that you own nothing. Absolutely nothing. Everything belongs to life.

And now slowly, begin to acknowledge all the things that life has given you. Everything you have received.

Begin to look at each thing that life has given you, each person, each emotion.

And try to feel grateful for the countless things you have received.

Allow that gratitude to grow in your heart. Allow it to invade your energy with its extraordinary frequency.

And you will never perceive life in the same way again.

JESUS

107

Dependency

Do not be dependent.

This is the secret.

Do not be dependent.

Think about this. Think about a day in which you feel so connected, so content, so satisfied with your own emotions, and so fulfilled, merely because you are now free and no longer need to try to live up to other people's expectations, that you finally feel at peace.

And your life moves peacefully toward infinity.

Does this mean you no longer wish for anything?

Does it mean you no longer dream?

Not at all.

You have wishes, dreams, you long for things to keep improving.

So what has changed?

What is the difference between the times in which you desired things to fill the void you felt and to make you feel safe and now, when you have accepted your spiritual dimension but continue to want the things from down there?

It is simple.

We are no longer talking about a need.

What I mean by this is that you now feel complete; you no longer need those things. Your happiness is no longer dependent on them.

Now, if they happen to come along, great. It's perfectly normal for you to like them, but you are no longer emotionally dependent on them, you no longer feel that you cannot live without them.

Do you see the difference?

Do this exercise.

Focus on what you want. Then think about how you would feel if you could not have this, whether you feel good without necessarily feeling that this thing completes you. If you feel content, simply because of the pleasure this thing gives you, congratulations, it means that you are no longer emotionally dependent on things that are outside of yourself.

However, if the possibility of never getting what you want makes you feel down and dejected, if you feel as if the world is over, be wary.

Your inner self is empty; your essence is weeping and needs urgent spiritual care.

JESUS

108

Being Afraid

There is something you want, yet it scares you.

Part of you wants it; the other part of you is afraid.

You are afraid of the risk; you are afraid of delving into the unknown.

What should you do?

First and foremost:

Understand why you want it. Why do you need this wish to come true? So that you will be accepted? So that you can feel safer? So that you can be happier? To get rid of your feelings of dissatisfaction?

Contemplate this: only that which comes from within can bring you complete happiness.

The secret is: every time you want to do something just because you feel bad, find a way to cheer yourself up. Find a way to make yourself feel better. Meditate, go to therapy, come up to heaven, cry, or do something that will make you feel better inside.

Then, once you feel better, once you feel balanced and happy, ask yourself, "Do I really want to pursue this matter?"

At this point you have already chosen.

If the answer is no, it is because you were looking for something outside yourself to make you feel better inside. Obviously, that was never going to work, for you were running away and avoiding the root of the problem.

By forcing yourself to feel better through meditation, looking deep within yourself, or whatever it is you do, you are validating one of the highest principles of heaven.

Everything is cured from the inside out, from within outward, not the other way round.

If the answer was "no," you managed to avoid a procedure that would have been a complete waste of time.

However, if you answered "yes," if you still wish to pursue this regardless of feeling better, that is a different thing altogether.

We are talking about intuition. We are talking about communication with heaven. We are talking about something that is in harmony with your original energy.

You may move forward, for no matter how difficult the journey is, it will never divert you from your original path. On the contrary, it will end up playing a part in the enrichment of your inner self.

JESUS

109

Condolences

The only thing I can say to you is "My condolences."

My condolences for your not yet knowing who you are, for your not listening to yourself, for your not respecting yourself, and for your misleading yourself.

Misleading yourself about the type of person you think you are or would like to be.

It is all a mask, it is all mechanical.

The fact that you do not internalize things is much more harmful than you can ever imagine.

The fact that you never reach inside, especially into your chest, where your heart beats and your feelings gush out . . .

The fact that you never get in contact with what is most intimate within you, the most profound part of your being . . .

The fact that you have never gotten in touch with your essence, that most profound and enlightened being that resides at the core of you . . .

The fact that you never listen to your inner voice, the one in which you will find the flame of eternal life, which does not fade away with physical life . . .

The fact that you do not delve into the depths of your own life to gain spiritual knowledge of what is truly good or bad for you . . .

The very fact that you do not look to me, never entrust me with anything to look after or protect.

The fact that you never ask me questions so that you can then look to life for the answers . . .

The fact that you never do any of these things makes me cry bitterly.

But it also gives me hope that as a result of feeling so dissatisfied, of not knowing why things happen to you, not feeling supported or protected, feeling a knot in your chest and not having the slightest idea as to where to begin . . . I really believe that because of all this, you will one day look at me.

And you will feel that I love you.

JESUS

110
Taking Risks

Bigger risks may attract bigger rewards.

Every risk you take may end in glory or in failure.

It all depends on how you face those risks.

Whether you advance from the outside in, from a materialistic perspective, in terms of what you will gain. Or whether you face risk in a controlled manner, accessing beforehand all the benefits you may reap.

If you advance entirely focused on the outcome, it is obvious that nothing will happen, given that you are focusing your energy on the end result rather than on the action itself.

Clearly, here, you are focusing on the future.

This future does not belong to you, and it does not like to be pressured, construed, or controlled.

And given that your expectations regarding the outcome are so high, it is only natural that you will suffer disappointment when reality forces the results to take a turn for the worse.

Looking at things from another angle:

When you take risks because you are greatly inspired; when it truly comes from within; when you are in the present and the future asks you to take risks . . .

When you are so completely centered that you do not even consider steering clear of risk . . .

When you understand that the society you live in and the people who are part of it will not live a minute longer without your achievements . . .

Regardless of how small or big the risk is, if you wish to go ahead with it for us, the people of heaven, so that we can reach people more easily . . .

If taking risks means you are opening up paths, enlightening souls, comforting hearts, giving meaning to life, touching people, and if this essentially makes you happy . . .

Go ahead. It is time. Everything will come together in harmony.

Take the risk. It has always been the best and biggest risks that have built great bridges for the future.

JESUS

111

Sensitivity

Activate your sensitivity. Activate your supreme sensitivity.

So that you can feel everything around you.

So that you can recognize the signs. So that you realize that the signs are not visible since they take place mainly within your energetic system.

Feel things as profoundly as possible. Cry if you need to, but cry from emotion. Crying is not always about pain.

Activate your supreme sensitivity so that you can understand what is happening. For what is happening is beyond words, sound, or shape.

What is happening is pure energy.

Activate your supreme sensitivity.

Accept it. To be sensitive is a gift.

And when you recognize yourself as the sensitive human being you are, only then ascend.

Receive my energy and my blessing.

And you will see how from this point forward, life will cease to be such a mystery.

JESUS

112

The Soul

One day, a little soul up in heaven decided to reincarnate. It was a very bright flame of light, up in the clouds, waiting to incarnate.

It had ascended some time before and had spent a while analyzing the past, a past life—past lives, to be more precise. Analyzing everything it had achieved and all that it had fallen short of, insufferable emotions it had cleansed and others it had gained.

This little soul, up in the clouds, was getting ready for a new journey. It was also preparing its mission, choosing what it would do this time round and the demands it would be subjected to in order to succeed in its new task.

It went on to choose the style of country, the type of parents, and its economic, social, and environmental circumstances.

Whether it would be born extremely sensitive or with a huge emotional blockage.

Everything was planned down to the very last detail, alongside the other souls that it would later cross paths with. On incarnating and entering the body of a newborn, it would forget everything. The cloak of forgetfulness is unrelenting. There was one thing that it was asked not to forget, one thing only. "You may forget everything we planned. You may even fail in your mission, block out your emotions and fail to evolve. But we ask you to remember one thing: do not forget that you must not, under any circumstances, allow your light to go out. Whatever happens, do not allow it to go out."

This is your story.

I know you have forgotten it all. But I also know that you have not forgotten what is essential.

Do whatever it takes to keep your light from going out.

JESUS

113

The Three Dimensions

Each of you has three dimensions.

Each of you vibrates with the energy from the triangle in these three dimensions: the mental dimension, the emotional dimension, and the spiritual dimension, or, in other words, the soul's dimension.

You will reach harmony only when you can vibrate equally in all three dimensions.

This is not happening, however. This is not how it has been.

Lately, human beings have been vibrating through the mental dimension.

This dimension controls the other two.

When you are sad, you think, "How silly, I feel sad and have no idea why." And you try to stop feeling sad.

In reality, you are using your mind to manipulate your emotions.

You are saying to your pain, "Stop hurting because I don't understand where you are coming from."

And you close up.

And in doing so, you halt the emotional flux that would have almost certainly taken you somewhere.

When you feel the calling, when you feel the energy from Aquarius, when you get emotional over coincidences, over events that are unusual and enlightening, when you see life passing before you, when you feel the light, and even when you feel me, the first thing you think is "There I go, making things up. There I go, hallucinating."

And you cut things short. You hold back.

That is your mind stopping your spiritual dimension from manifesting itself.

Because you are energy, and that is all you are. And energy manifests itself.

You have three dimensions.

Do not allow your mental dimension to dominate. Harmonize.

Think. And think things through.

Feel. And respect what you feel.
Be intuitive and follow your light.
And you will be harmonious.
You will be balanced.
You will be happy.

JESUS

114

My Love for You

Have I ever told you that I love you?

That I feel what you feel?

That I miss you; miss having you close to me?

Have I ever told you that I miss not having you around, that I miss your light?

Have I ever told you about what we went through up here together, before you incarnated?

We experienced so many things when we were one, fused, when we were together.

It is not the same up here without you.

Things are not the same without your light, without your desire to descend to earth to incarnate and continue with your mission toward evolution.

Have I told you that I await your return so that you may take a break from your evolutional suffering and we can play together once more, shine together again?

Naturally, I want you to remain on earth for many, many years.

Needless to say, only God knows when you will be back. But I want you to know that you are also needed up here. And no matter how long it takes, I am waiting for you to give you a kiss of light.

JESUS

115
Pact

If you are unable to do what you need to do out of an unequivocal respect for the person you are, do it for me. For the unconditional love that I have for you and for all those who are part of your race.

First, do things for yourself—through me.

Then, as you begin to feel the pleasant winds of change, you will begin to understand. You will begin to yield. You will find yourself as long as you are free, as long as you are true to yourself.

Have I ever told you I love you?

That I feel what you feel?

That what hurts you hurts me? Regardless of knowing that you are in pain, I cannot choose for you nor alleviate your pain.

Unless it is through these words.

I love you for taking responsibility for your life and for your energy.

I love you for knowing that the situation you find yourself in is a consequence of your previous choices.

I love you for entrusting yourself to heaven and to your own heart, putting everything else aside.

I love you for feeling and for feeling me.

Recognize how valuable our relationship is and make this pact with me.

You will then slowly get used to doing things on your own, for yourself.

That is the moment of your essence. It is a time when you find your most infinite inspirations.

It is when everything makes sense again and you begin to understand the motives for having traveled the wide-open roads that brought you here.

JESUS

116

Your Love for Me

This is your love for me.

When you look at yourself in the mornings and once again try to accept who you are.

This is your love for me. When you nourish your body properly to avoid falling sick.

This is your love for me. When you offer yourself small gifts just because you deserve it. Because I deserve that you deserve it.

When you become wise.

When you reach me up in heaven.

When you dream about me and smile at me.

This is your love for me.

I don't want you to write.

I only want you to feel, to feel that love for me (the love you feel for me).

Every lake you look at, you look at for me.

Every sunset, every shooting star you contemplate, share some of that pleasure with me.

Every memory you have, have it for me.

Do it for me.

Every person you hug and each gaze you connect with, do it for me.

Love for me.

I cannot be there, but I experience that moment through each of you, through every human being who honors what he feels. Who sees his heart soaring toward the sky.

Every time you fall in love, do it for me.

Every time you use my light to love, contemplate, and live, you will feel more of yourself, you will give more, and you will unify heaven and earth through the strength of our union.

JESUS

117
Death

Do not fear death, my child, for everything is as it should be.

Death is but another life. The platonic transformation between heaven and earth.

Transformation and learning, effort and conviction are all part of the human soul.

You die with the passing of each day, as each day becomes yesterday.

Only to be reborn the very next day.

JESUS

118

The Search

Stop searching for me at altars, in prayers, and in processions.

I am here.

I am no longer the one who you worship, that mournful image.

I am alive, and I am here.

I am here as energy, in a new dimension.

In a dimension that you will have to explore and brave if you wish to be with me.

If you truly wish to be with me.

It has been a long time since I was last in that dimension.

I am no longer there.

At least not this I, the "I" that I wish you to be acquainted with.

This I, who is more complete and less temporal.

This I, who is more vibrant, energetic, and intense.

This I of light.

Stop looking for me on the outside.

I am here.

Right here, deep inside you.

And every time you look within yourself, you will see me.

And you will realize that I am no longer in those paintings in antique frames or in the cathedrals.

I am here inside you, as energy, to help you discover yourself and to feel, deeply feel, who you truly are.

JESUS

119
Mission

Your mission is part of each and every day.

What does this mean?

Let me explain.

There are some of you who believe that your mission on earth has to be great. A large part of you believes that your mission should essentially be a professional task. And many of you believe that you will discover your mission if you follow the signs, which is not altogether wrong.

But the signs I speak of are not external signs, they are not something that happens to you, they are not something you suddenly remember.

A sign is, above all, something you feel.

The truth is that none of you knows what your mission is.

Not even you.

Your mission on earth is something intrinsic, so deep within that it can never begin on the outside.

It can never begin in matter.

It has to be born within.

It can never start off in your head or your mind.

It has to begin in your heart.

And moreover, it has to have a format.

Look at Alexandra, for example.

As a result of a loss she suffered, she decided that what she needed first and foremost was to get to know herself. She believed that if we attract what we emanate, the fact that she had attracted this specific loss could only mean that she was emanating something strange.

She went on to learn how to change that energy. Later on, she began trying to teach others how to change their energy.

Meanwhile, she continued to change her own energy.

Then, during her search, she found me. She made a commitment to follow me. And today we have our project.

Do you understand how things work?

The search begins from within.

Trying to discover who you are.

Trying to change that energy.

Trying to ascend.

If you vow to take this path to self-discovery, sooner or later you will find your essence.

It will grow in strength, self-esteem, and confidence, and it will steer you toward that which was planned for you on earth.

You will start off slowly, looking each person in the eye, looking yourself in the eye, giving love and affection to everyone who crosses your path—going through your own mourning process so that you may remove it from your heart and become a truly caring person.

And during this process of self-discovery and of giving love—to yourself and others—one day, when you least expect it, you will be at the heart of your mission.

Enjoy your journey.

JESUS

120
Attitude

Your mission is an attitude.

Your mission is not a road, it is not a path.

Your mission is not a profession, and it does not require you to build on anything.

Neither is it a person nor a trace of anyone.

Your mission is an attitude. It is something that you practice every day from the privacy of your home to the way you live in society.

It is an attitude, small and subtle.

It starts off slowly.

Making eye contact when you talk to people. Touching them, hugging your friends, and treating those you love with respect.

Never raising your voice to anyone.

All this is part of your mission.

People think that their mission is something great, something extraordinary and wonderful.

It may even turn out to be so.

If you hug people more often and look deeper into their eyes.

If you intensify the love you have for others.

If you build caring and loving communities.

Then you will have a great mission ahead of you.

You do not discover your mission by thinking.

You discover your mission by feeling.

And it is in the smallest of things that you will find the path that will one day help you to become a being who lights the way for others.

JESUS

121

The Person You Have Turned Into

Look at the type of person you have turned into.

More caring, more tolerant, and more compassionate.

Think of how you used to be.

Closed, hard, and defiant.

Look how far you have come.

Recognize how much you have already done at an emotional level.

Obviously, you aren't finished. It is clear that you have not yet arrived at your goal.

But is there really a place you need to arrive at?

Matter is dual. There are always opposites. The perfect and imperfect exist hand in hand throughout eternity. We are talking not about perfect beings but about less resistant beings.

That is, in fact, the authentic path.

And the less resistant you are, the more open you will be emotionally.

Cry when you need to cry.

Laugh out loud when you need to laugh.

Live each emotion to the fullest, without judgment.

You are getting closer, aren't you?

Look at the person you have turned into. And notice how I become stronger every time you become a better person.

JESUS

122

Extreme Sensitivity

Be sensitive. That is all.

That is all I ask for.

I ask you to be more sensitive so that all that belongs to heaven may flow through your body, through your being, in the truest way possible.

I ask you to be sensitive, to accept that you are sensitive, for this is the direction people must take in order to find their own true path.

Naturally, it is the longest path.

Naturally, it is the purest path.

The one that no one has thought of, no one has subtracted, no one has thought out.

The path to extreme sensitivity is the path of angels who descend to earth to help people advance.

And you may well be that angel. You simply do not remember.

JESUS

123

Give to Yourself

I do not want to receive what you wish to give me.

Do you know why?

Because you do not give yourself anything.

You want to give me everything.

And do you know something?

I cannot receive anything unless it has come through your essence.

If you do not give yourself anything, you are not giving me anything.

I need things with soul. It is with your soul that you communicate with me.

Everything you do for me lacks soul, because it does not come through you, through your filter, through your soul.

Everything you are going through at the moment has a name:

Lack of essence.

The Universe takes from you so that you will look inside yourself.

Never forget this.

JESUS

124
Your Love

Give them love.

Give all of your love.

Your deepest love.

Your most intrinsic love.

Communicate your love.

Express your love physically.

Tell people how much you love them.

Touch, kiss, hug, speak.

At every moment, at each and every occasion in your life, love and express that love.

Touch all the people who cross your path.

Touch and pass on energy.

Look and pass on energy.

Smile and pass on energy.

Become enlightened and send out hope.

Your whole life will begin to transform with that touch, that look, that smile, and that light.

The whole of the Universe will change a little because of your attitude.

The whole of the Universe will change a little because you chose to change.

The whole of the Universe will change a little because you chose to love.

And I, way up here, so far away, will receive the energy that you have chosen to emanate.

And I, way up here, will receive the love you have chosen to give.

JESUS

125
Farewell

Let it go—whatever it is that is at stake.

Let it go, beyond eternity.

Let it go.

Let everything go. Every bond, every particle. Let them leave.

Say good-bye. Say good-bye.

We will see each other later up in heaven.

Time does not exist. We will meet shortly.

Space does not exist. We will see each other soon.

Let it go.

Let it loose.

Let it be reborn.

So that it may grow once more.

Let it go slowly toward heaven.

Slowly, like the sound of a clarinet playing.

Slowly, the way your heart beats.

Slowly . . . slower . . . slower . . . slower . . .

JESUS

126
Knowing I Am Here

I am with you, always.

Every minute of your day and of your night.

Throughout all the difficult periods in which you think you are alone—think again.

I am here. Always. Inside your heart, wrapping you in soft, white energy. With this love.

Somber times are always times of solitude. They are learning periods.

And I am here, always near you, guiding you through your intuition.

You receive my guidance and transmit what you receive from me.

This is our communion.

I am here. I have always been here.

And knowing you believe this will bring me so much peace.

JESUS

127
Gratitude

Imagine that you do not expect anything from life. You receive what life has to offer you . . . and that is all.

Imagine that at some point something is wrong. Naturally, you feel sad.

You don't get angry, for only those who believe they have a right to something get angry.

And you know that down there, in matter, you have a right only to what you conquer energetically. And that is all.

Imagine that something good happens to you. As you know you played no hand in it, you thank heaven.

Gratitude is a sentiment that elevates you.

When you are elevated and feel thankful, you attract only good fortune.

You simply attract greater abundance.

When a person believes he has played a part in this, he feels so proud, he focuses so hard on the force that allowed him to succeed, that he overexerts his ego, which, already being so dense, only ends up attracting more density.

This is why man usually goes on to suffer great defeat shortly after he has achieved great success.

That is why those who do not go in search of anything normally attain everything.

JESUS

128

Rupture

No matter how much you reject it, rupture exists and needs to be dissected.

When is someone on the verge of rupture? When he has used up all his opportunities, when he has gone astray from his path, or when time has run out.

In your case, you have used up all your opportunities, you have strayed from your path, and time has run out.

It is over. It happened. It is the past.

The present and the future have nothing to do with the past.

The past has nothing to do with who you are today.

Cut. Dissect. Understand.

Then take a leap forward. Move forward with conviction so that you can complete what has yet to be accomplished.

JESUS

129
Martyr

A martyr is someone who suffers because I suffered.

And those who suffer believe they are closer to me. In suffering, they believe, they are creating empathy with me and I will become closer to them out of pity or compassion.

This is not the way things work.

I am the first to tell you that you should cry when you are feeling sad. I am also the first to tell you that you should not run from pain. When it comes, you should face it and express your grief.

To grieve is to cry, to let your feelings out and to cleanse.

Remove all density from your chest.

This is what you should do.

Martyrs seek pain.

They believe that pain purifies; therefore, they seek pain so that they may be purified.

And they believe that I will thank them for this. I will not thank them. I will not even go near them. Those who turn themselves into martyrs are victims. They seek attention; they want to be greater and better than others.

Those who turn themselves into martyrs want to be the first to reach heaven.

And what if I told you that it is easy to become a martyr and that being happy in the midst of all that density on earth is much harder?

And what if I told you that people need to treat themselves well and make choices that make them grow rather than choices that diminish them? And what if I told you that those who look after themselves look after their essence, and only a healthy essence will open up to let me in?

Think about it.

Suffering is constructive only when the pain is yours and you decide to confront it, not because you wish to be a martyr but because you wish to cleanse it forever so that it will never return.

Think about who you are and not who I, up here, would like you to be. Think about who you would like to be, a unique, original, and abundant being.

And I am sure that this being would not gain happiness through seeking pain.

JESUS

130
A Third Way

I have been telling you what you have to do.

Sometimes the things I tell you to do are difficult; other times they are unimaginable.

I tell you to do things that are plain and simple or complex and essential.

And of course you try to do them. That is clear.

But you do not always succeed.

You are not always able to. You have not always evolved enough to do so.

And this is where guilt steps in.

"I didn't do this, I didn't do that. I didn't do what I was supposed to do."

Guilt.

From here on, you are faced with two problems:

Not having done what I asked you to do, which naturally causes your soul some embarrassment . . .

And feeling guilty for not having done what I asked, which naturally causes me some embarrassment.

But this is not the issue.

And what if you were to find a third way of doing things instead of doing what I ask and then feeling guilty for having failed?

A more feasible way?

If I ask you to run a hundred meters and you are unable to do so, what would be more advantageous? Not to run at all or to run fifty, sixty, seventy meters? Or maybe twenty or thirty?

To run some distance, at least.

In this case, the more you run, regardless of whether or not you manage a hundred meters, I repeat, the more you run, the closer you get to your original destination, the one I have picked out.

Now think about the things I ask you of you.

Some are impossible for you.

Impossible, for now.

Because if you start doing part of these things now and keep going in that direction, you will become closer to my objective.

For example, you may not be able to forgive someone, but you may treat that person more lovingly.

You may not be able to treat him lovingly, but you can treat him with more respect.

There is always something you can do.

Never forget: every step we take toward the light is a step we take away from the darkness.

JESUS

131

Entrust

You can learn something only if what you are learning is in harmony with your energy.

In order to learn something that has a higher energy, you have to choose to open up your energy at a higher level.

Everything happens this way, even the learning process.

You say, "All knowledge is self-knowledge." And I say, naturally, because you can understand only what you can absorb with your energy.

You do not take in anything that is not in harmony with your energy. It does not enter.

You have to open up. You have to open your heart and allow it to ascend to higher vibrations.

Guilt, judgment, and fear close your heart.

Unconditional love opens it.

Come up here. Meditate. Convene with the light. Surrender to the light.

Recognize that here in heaven there may exist a vast, protective, friendly light, which helps and protects you, not necessarily with what you want but with what is good for you.

Acknowledge that you may receive protection from this light, as long as you entrust yourself to it.

Entrust. And your energy will rise.

And from here on out, you will understand and learn things more deeply.

JESUS

132

My Light

It is obvious that you need my light.

Come and find me so that you may calm yourself.

Look for me in the calmness of the sea, in the starlight, in the volcano's fury.

Look for me in the never-ending fields, in the ever-changing flowers, and in the noise of the rain.

Discover me in the ocean's depths and in the many species that exist. Look for me in nature.

And if you do not find me, it is because your eyes are not yet ready to see me.

So close your eyes and look inward.

Look at yourself.

See yourself.

Recognize yourself. Love yourself.

And naturally, I will be there.

JESUS

133

The Voice

Do what your intuition tells you to do.

Learn to understand where your intuition takes you.

It is the greatest current in your life.

It is the voice, the command. It knows what is good for you.

And when everyone thinks that you have gone mad, that you no longer have control, that you no longer have objectives . . .

When they think that you have given in, that you are no longer putting up a resistance and are doing things the wrong way around . . .

You are going to feel a light growing in your heart.

And that light will be so strong, so powerful, and so solid and conscious, that light will be so completely yours, that perhaps for the first time in your life you will understand what it means to be happy.

JESUS

134

Knowing You Have Nothing

You have nothing. Nothing in matter is yours. Nothing at all.

You have no father or mother.

They are simply souls who accompany you on this journey. They descended with you to share. Not to possess.

You have no children. You have no family, no friends.

They are all souls, souls who gather in the clouds so that they may incarnate together with one purpose and in one direction.

They do not belong to you. They never will.

Nor do you belong to them. Never. Ever.

Think about how liberating it is not to possess anything or anyone. Think about how simple life becomes.

To see objects and people as being autonomous, free from your energy.

Free from your overbearing attachment.

Ask yourself, "If I do not love anything and nothing belongs to me, what is all this that surrounds me? Who do these things belong to? Whom do these people belong to?"

The answer:

They belong to life. Life bequeathed them to you during your brief passage on earth.

They are a gift from heaven, something to take pleasure in, to make the most of, to enjoy, to share, and, above all, to learn from and let go of.

Always remember what I have told you: "I love you regardless of where you are in physical life."

And on the day you understand that nothing belongs to you and life gives you everything, you will finally begin to feel gratitude.

You will feel grateful for all that surrounds you, grateful for the gifts that life gives you, grateful for realizing that all this has logic, grateful for your awareness.

And when you experience a feeling of gratitude that is so intense that it almost makes your heart burst open, ascend. Come up here.

Gratitude is the most fulfilling way of reaching me.

JESUS

135
Help

I know you like to help. I know you try hard. You want to convey all you know to others, everything you have learned from me.

And you believe this is reasonable. I understand. You do what you know and believe is right. You do not question it. You do not consider, even for a moment, that this enormous gift may be your ego at work. You never think about this.

I understand.

Even though you may have believed up until this moment that this was acceptable, once you read this message you will realize it is not. And the logic is simple.

Pay attention:

When you decide to help someone, how do you go about it?

You feel sorry for that person. You think he or she is going through a difficult time, so you come up with a way of getting him or her out of that situation.

Completely justifiable, you think to yourself.

I understand why you think this way. But it doesn't really work like this.

You need to understand that the strategy you came up with to help this individual bears your own logic. It has your energy and your energy alone. It doesn't bear that person's energy—or, to be more precise, this person does not possess the energy of the strategy you developed for him or her.

That's why it is extremely unlikely that he or she will be able to put it into practice. And even if he or she does, it is extremely unlikely that the problem will be resolved.

Why?

Because whenever someone does something that doesn't have their energy, later on, when he has to face the consequences and make daily decisions that are based on this strategy, he will be unable to understand the logic behind it.

Hence, he will be unable to make decisions based on that strategy and, as a result, the problem will not be resolved. Why do I say that it is the ego at work when you use this method to help others?

Because only the ego wants to impose its logic on others. The soul does not impose anything on others, yet it helps them.

The soul looks at the person who stands before it. The soul deeply feels that person.

The soul is able to determine where that person's soul lies.

It can draw it out. And it helps this person to free himself from fear, and once free from fear he can make choices based on his own logic.

This is what helping is about. It is not about making decisions, giving opinions, or solving other people's problems for them.

Real help is about getting the other person's soul to shine by means of compassion, cleansing, and love.

And as I often say, the best thing you can do for someone who is not well, besides cleansing, is to say "I know you can do it."

And the following day, call him up, perhaps to cleanse him again, and repeat those words until the soul manifests itself.

Until that person succeeds.

This is what it means to help someone.

JESUS

136
Today Is the Day

Today is the day to do something completely different from what you are used to doing. This is not the day for fortitude or for calming the masses, for praying, going out, or sharing your feelings. Today you should neither lie in the sun nor reflect on the law.

This is not the day for speaking out or calling out to the heavens.

Today is not for running. It is a day for stopping.

Motionless. Just like that. Sad. That is right. This is the day to be, to just be in this immense world and to flutter on the edge of my hand.

Today is the day to revere the master, to worship your energy.

This is the day for showing your gratitude by doing favors for others.

This is the day for looking at time and admiring infinity.

A day to simply allow your heart to beat.

Today is the day for all that is subjective on this earth.

That which has no name.

That which has no age.

That which has no form.

Today is the day for something that only those who have been there—only those who have felt and those who have reached—can understand.

JESUS

137
Ties

Have I ever told you what we have in common?

Energy.

And do you know what energy does?

It vibrates.

We both vibrate, although at different frequencies.

You still vibrate in the frequency of primary emotions such as fear, regret, and guilt.

I vibrate in a much higher frequency of sentiment and universal love.

And why are you unable to vibrate in the same type of frequency as me? Why are you unable to reach me at this level of vibration?

Why aren't you here?

On account of one simple word. A concept: salvation.

Because of that word, you are going to remain down there even longer. Bound to the wheel of incarnations. Bound to the ties you have.

But if you really think about it, you do not really want to leave.

So what if I told you that I would rescue you and bring you here, close to me, but if and only if you changed vibration?

And what if I told you that you could come, but if and only if you gave something up . . . would you come?

And what if I told you that in order to elevate your vibrational frequency, to step out of the wheel of incarnations and come live eternally at my side you would need to do one thing and one thing only . . . would you come?

Well, it is simple.

All you have to do is give up everything you are attached to and let go of all ties.

Detach yourself from those you love and those you hate.

Detach yourself from people and things, emotions, feelings, worries, pain, density, conflict, rivalry, competitiveness and envy, living on the edge, impropriety, emancipation, flesh, skin, and heart.

Detach from the world, from life.

Detach from the love that exists down there.

Detach from everything.

Would you come?

Since I know the answer is no, I implore you to begin slowly detaching yourself from everything that you love so that you may become closer to Paradise.

JESUS

138

Blessings

Look upon the good things that happen to you as gifts from me.

Think of them as gifts.

Consider that your life is neutral and that these things are offerings from heaven.

They are blessings.

Look upon the good things that happen to you as blessings that I bestow upon you.

For your commitment.

For your perseverance.

For your faith.

And if you think in this way, you will begin to feel gratitude.

A feeling of gratitude that is so great, so intense, and so profound that it will almost certainly change your energy.

It will take it higher.

You will feel lighter. You will feel more uplifted.

And when you ascend higher up, up here, I will have the opportunity to hug you myself.

JESUS

139

Masks

Stop lying to yourself.

You have invented a persona that you want everyone to accept so they won't be able to see who you really are.

Why do you want to hide?

Why do you not like yourself?

I want you to know that we up here deal only with the truth.

You can hide your true self from everyone else.

You can even hide it from yourself.

But you will never be able to hide it from me.

I vibrate through truth. And by vibrating through truth, I attract truth.

By constantly hiding yourself from others, you have gone into hiding from yourself.

You no longer know who you are.

You no longer know who you could be.

As I have often told you, "Discover what the Universe wants from you, and make this your main priority."

At this moment, the Universe wants you to remove these masks you have created and that fail to reflect who you are, and to put everything on hold so that you may begin to work out who you are.

JESUS

140

Priorities

Learn to recognize what is at the core of your heart.

At any time, you have a number of priorities.

They may be professional, familial, or of the heart.

However, I never seem to see people with emotional priorities.

An emotional priority is something that you have to experience regardless of whether it is good or bad, pretty or ugly. It doesn't matter what form it takes.

For your soul to continue toward evolution, for it to keep going at a steady pace, you need to experience different emotions. To unblock. To liberate yourself. To keep moving forward.

Do this:

Think of a situation that has been repeating itself for some time.

What emotion does it provoke in you?

Have you covered up or blocked out this emotion? Have you allowed yourself to dissolve in a sea of tears each time it appears, which may be poignant but is not really liberating?

Blocking out an emotion when it arises could be the reason why these situations keep repeating themselves.

This is your emotional priority. Now is the time to try to unearth this emotion, for it may well be hidden. You have not paid it the attention it deserves.

Go to your heart.

Learn to see what is inside, at its core.

Accept that emotion.

Cry.

Open your heart, and let the negative energy out.

And then calm yourself.

When we accept our priorities, everything begins to fall into place and life becomes a pleasure rather than a sea of confusion.

Your emotional priorities are your most important priorities.

After all, they are lodged in your heart, which is your most sacred place.

JESUS

141

The Next Task

I am going to dictate your next task.

Your next task is to learn to vibrate through the person you are.

Without disguises, without deceit, without airs and graces.

The next task, regardless of the question you have asked—and you may ask this question again later, at another time—is to be yourself.

Without deviations or omissions, without outbursts of childish opportunism, without trying to smooth matters over.

To be who you really are demands total commitment.

To be your true self and to respect what you feel will demand a lot of energy from you at this stage in your life.

This could be because you have never respected your essence and it is now time to change the direction of things or because you have been practicing a lot and it is now time to take that giant leap.

Only you can say which it is . . . well, you and I, of course.

So listen carefully to what I am going to tell you: Close this book. Focus on your heart, and feel. Just feel. That is all.

And the more you get used to feeling without focusing on anything, the quicker you will connect to your soul and finally discover who you are and what you are doing here.

JESUS

142

Biological Clock

There are times when you want to do the things you have been dreaming of for so long.

Other times you feel frustrated because you cannot do the things that you have long been dreaming of.

What is wrong here?

What is wrong is the lack of respect you are showing for your biological clock.

What you have been dreaming of for so long may be past its deadline.

What you have been dreaming of for so long should have been realized a long time ago. The fact that you did not carry it through at that time does not mean you should do it now, outside its time limit.

If you try to realize today what you dreamt of some time ago, you may end up ignoring what you are currently dreaming of.

A dream has a specific time limit. Your biological clock summons it.

Your organs and cells are coordinated to extract the best experiences for your evolutional process from this dream.

If you try to realize this dream at a later date, it will be nothing more than a mirage. Your energy is not synchronized to make it happen, and to try to carry it through will only end in frustration.

Close your eyes. Meditate. Try to feel what your biological clock wants from you at present.

Forget your old dreams. Focus on your new dreams.

Focus on what you can be, do, and think and the way in which you can proceed when connected to your energy's current alignment.

And whatever emerges from this will be a new dream. And you will have all the resources to make it come true.

JESUS

143

Tiredness

Tiredness is a sign.

Either you are on the wrong path, or you are going too fast on the right path.

The important thing is to focus. Whether you are trying to find your bearings or change speed, the important thing is to center yourself.

Stop. Do not be afraid of stopping. Stop often, and at different intervals, to breathe. To breathe and feel the present.

Those who are on the wrong path do not feel the path they are on. They are interested only in arriving.

Those who are going too fast do not feel the path. They are interested only in arriving.

When those on the wrong path arrive, they feel extremely disappointed because their destination does not merit what they had to go through to get there.

This is to be expected, given that the wrong path will ultimately lead to the wrong destination.

Those who are going too fast will never reach their destination because they will tumble before they get there.

As you can see, regardless of which situation you find yourself in, the journey is unsatisfactory.

And when the journey is not satisfactory, it is best to stop.

Stop. Breathe. Remain where you are. And take care of the present, become centered, so that tomorrow your legs will have more energy to make the most of each step of the journey that remains.

JESUS

144
Coming Up Here

How are you getting on in your spirituality?

Do you come up here in search of something?

Do you come up here to receive something?

Some sort of blessing?

Do you come here to show gratitude for something you have received?

Or do you come to be?

To be who you are in a new dimension?

If you come here in search of something, stop. You will not find what you are looking for here.

The most you will find is the answer—to whether or not you are going to find what you want.

If you come to show your gratitude, that is wonderful. I am pleased that you realize that everything you receive in matter is sent by heaven as a gesture of goodwill. On the other hand, if you come to be, to practice being who you are, I will be so overwhelmingly happy that I will have them sound the trumpets. It means that you have arrived at the portal of dimensions, because you have received enough light to enable you to choose the light.

It means that you have forgiven yourself and no longer make demands on yourself. For you have chosen to experience all of your pain alongside all of your love, and you already know who I am and the good I can bring you.

It means that you understand this journey man is on and you want to do your part.

It means you think of me, and even though you may not yet have seen me, you know I exist and that you can count on me.

It means that you have delivered your soul to heaven and you await glad tidings.

And above all, it means that your soul has already touched mine.

JESUS

145
Advice

A piece of advice for you:

Try to be someone your essence would be proud of.

Try to be the way it would like you to be.

Your essence is the most intimate part of you. It is the purest energy.

When you are something it can be proud of, it is a sign that you are already in touch with your essence, that you know and respect what your essence is.

And you want to be like your essence because you recognize that this energy is unique and undistorted.

When you try to be someone else, your essence becomes sad, downhearted, and withdrawn. When you accept and forgive yourself, it becomes free, powerful, and crystalline. It lives longer and is able to fulfill more missions on earth.

You live happily because you know who you are and you know how to handle it.

And I, up above, watch another star shine. This is the connection between the mind, which is the high frequency of acceptance, and light, the high frequency of the essence.

Try to live the way your essence would like you to. You will live longer and be happier.

And as for the ego, that voice in your head that tells you not to take risks, not to move ahead, that says you are incapable, that it isn't worth it, simply reject this self-restrictive energy and send it up here.

We will sort it out.

JESUS

146

You Don't Need Anything Else

Everything that you have today is precisely what you need to move on to the next stage of your life. No more, no less.

That is all. Just that. What is at your disposal today is all you need. It is all you require to move on to the next stage.

You need only what you have, what is at your disposal.

Obviously, you would like more. This is natural. Of course you would like better circumstances (or so you think) in order to reach your objectives faster.

The first question I put to you is:

Do you really need to go faster?

Don't you think that you are able to empower, consolidate, and structure yourself better at the pace at which you are moving now?

Don't you think you have already attracted the exact speed at which you need to be moving so as to consistently rise above your struggles?

Would you be able to overcome your resistances if you were moving at a faster pace?

And my last question for you is:

Do you want everything to go faster so that you may reach your objectives quicker?

Which objectives?

Don't you think that on this slower, more restrictive path, you will be more willing to accept that those aren't your true objectives?

If you continue to want more, more things, at a faster rate, the time has arrived for you to cry over your powerlessness. Cry.

Cry over the fact that you have no say in the way things are. Cry because that is the only thing you can do at this moment.

Cry and come to terms with the fact that this is all you have right now. That is it.

And you do not need anything else.

Everything you have attracted, everything you have at your disposal, is exactly what you need to reach the next stage in your life.

To want more at this moment is to give voice to your ego.

And that is all I have to say to you.

JESUS

147

Mirror

What is inside is the same as what is on the outside.

This is a saying that you should keep in mind all your life.

Everything you attract outside of yourself is in fact inside you, deep within your heart.

So think about this:

How much violence do you attract? Is it physical violence or psychological violence?

How many people argue with you? How many mistreat you?

How many fail to listen to you? How many hurt your feelings?

How many stop you from moving forward? How many do not believe in you? How many fail to respect you? How many ignore you?

Be aware that everything that is done to you is a reflection of what you do to yourself.

Do not wish another person harm. Whoever did this to you is simply mirroring your inner self.

You harm yourself. You do not listen to yourself. You hurt your own feelings. You would like to advance beyond your means, in the best circumstances possible. You do not believe in or respect yourself. Last but not least, you ignore yourself.

Look at yourself. Stop looking at others. Stop focusing on what they do or fail to do for you.

Look at yourself and see the harm you have been doing to yourself by demanding so much from yourself . . . by wanting so much . . . by moving ahead so quickly . . . by being so intolerant with yourself . . . by not forgiving yourself.

Look at yourself, and pause for a while.

Stop. Feel. Be still.

Perhaps you will see a subtle, faint light, the light that belongs to your essence.

That light is simply waiting for you to look at it, instead of looking at others.

To value it, instead of valuing others.

And to love it.

And when you do, you will almost certainly attract true love.

JESUS

148
Blockage

When the journey is unfavorable, the more you strive to move forward, the harder the Universe tries to stop you.

When it is not yet time for something to happen, the more you strive to make it happen, the harder the Universe tries to block you.

When an issue is just starting to surface, the more you strive to speed it up, the more the Universe tries to hold you up so that things will have time to unfold.

The Universe is wise.

The energetic system is perfect.

And the ego ruins everything.

If something is energetically blocked, it is because mysterious forces know that this is not meant to happen.

At least not now.

But man insists. Insists. Keeps pushing forward. Insists. Insists. He wants it.

Consequently, he begins to attract all types of problems. From delays to insecurities, depression, accidents, sorrows, failures, betrayals, loss, illnesses, and so on.

And the ego looks at all this, cursing its bad luck.

It is unable to recognize that these are the consequences of its own actions, rather than actions themselves.

The ego is unable to understand why it attracts so much loss.

The ego is unable to understand that it attracts all this loss because of the force it puts into things.

The conscience however, understands. The soul understands. It is a question of expanding your conscience and yielding to your soul.

And you will come to understand that from up here, everything seems absolutely perfect.

And I will love you for realizing this.

With all my love.

JESUS

149

The Answer

Everything that happens in life has a purpose.

Everything that happens, even the tiniest things you attract, have a reason for being there, for happening precisely that way, at that specific moment, and in that exact place.

Everything there in matter is utterly perfect so that you, human beings, can respond accordingly.

In accordance with who you are, of course.

In accordance with who you choose to be in that situation, at that time, and in that location.

At this point you might ask, "How does a place such as the physical world, which is so dense and heavy, respond to such subtle impulses with such perfection?"

And the answer is simple:

You live in an energetic system, and this system functions at any frequency.

If someone is dense, he will attract dense people and situations via this energetic system. If someone is light, he will attract people and situations that are light.

It is simple, as everything is when seen from up here.

Therefore, and going back to what I said earlier, the situation you find yourself in at present is trying to tell you something. It is trying to show you things, to get you in touch with your emotions, to get you to change your belief system so that you will open your mind and believe in new opportunities, including new opportunities for you as a person.

The issue here is, What does all this mean?

Why do you find yourself in this situation?

What are you meant to learn from all this?

I may even be able to answer you from up here.

But in order for me to do so, you will have to come up here.

There is one thing that you must accept, and that is that you do not have the answer and you will not find it down there.

So do as I say: look for the answer in your Higher Self, or, if you still recall how, close your eyes, relax, and ask, "What is the Universe trying to tell me by way of this situation?"

Remain as you are. Empty. Do not focus on anything. Just ask the question.

And tune in to your sensibility. Be intuitive. Be perceptive.

You will believe that you are imagining things, but you are not.

That is the answer.

JESUS

150

Energetic Coherence

Who are you?

Are you your own person, or do you do what others want you to do?

Who are you, really?

Let me expand on this:

When someone hurts you, how do you react? Do you hurt him back?

When someone deceives you, what do you do? Do you also deceive? Do you attack? Do you argue? Do you intimidate? Are you judgmental? Do you blame others?

What I have to ask you is simple:

When someone hurts you and you hurt him back, why do you do it?

Because that is the type of person you are, someone who hurts others, or do you do it only because he has hurt you?

If you hurt someone because that is the way you are, that is something you choose to do. I can understand and can even say that I respect your choice, your essence's choice, the person you have chosen to be this time round.

And I respect it even though I do not agree with it. I do not agree with it, but I respect it. You are who you choose to be, and I cannot change that.

However, if you hurt people in retaliation because they have hurt you, if it is not a choice that comes from your essence, it is not who you are. If you do this only to "get back" at someone, we have a problem on our hands.

By getting back at someone, you fail to understand exactly what it is you are doing: You have descended to the level of the person who hurt you.

You move completely out of your energy.

You choose to be like that other person.

You enter into an unfamiliar energetic system, having no idea when you will go back to vibrating in your own essence.

Do you think this is how it should be?

Is this what you choose for yourself?

Be aware that there are times when we send you extremely dense experiences to measure your coherence.

Yet instead of being yourself at all times, you end up sailing on the waves of other people's energetic frequency: "I do this because they have done the same thing to me."

And so, with each action, you begin to simulate others without realizing how distant you have become from your true self, how far you are from the light, how far you are from finally returning home.

JESUS

151

Practice

What do you already know about the spiritual world?

What have you learned?

How often have you caught yourself correcting others because they did not act in accordance with what you believe?

How often have you caught yourself thinking about things in a different, more innovative way?

How often have you been surprised at yourself for going over concepts or reanalyzing situations from a spiritual perspective?

How often have you understood things in a new dimension?

I believe there have been plenty of times.

I think that your head is full of new concepts, new life strategies: "How do I do this, how should I react to that?"

But the question I put to you at this moment is this:

Have you put this into practice on a daily basis?

Are your actions in harmony with your newfound awareness, with your soul?

You know what to do and how to do it, but are you doing it?

Are you honoring the commitment you made with your soul?

Are you putting it into practice?

Think about your life.

Think about your day-to-day existence, from the moment you wake up to the moment you go to sleep.

Is there spiritual coherence?

Is there commitment?

Now is a good time to begin paying attention to the commitment you made to your soul.

To your commitment to your energy.

To your commitment to the future.

JESUS

152

Helping Others

Why do you have such a desire to help?

Why do you have this great need for others to be as you have idealized them?

Why do you try so hard to bring about this change?

Think about this:

If someone chooses not to change—or chooses to do what he or she wants and believes in—you will have to witness the consequences of those choices and as a result, you will have to watch that person suffer. And maybe he will be in so much pain that you will also end up suffering.

Going back to the first question:

Why do you have such a desire to help?

Because you do not want to suffer, you do not want to be affected by other people's pain.

That is but one of the helping rationales; the other is that helping others makes you feel powerful and wise. However, that is not the reason we are here today.

Do you want some advice? Do the following:

Change yourself. Focus on your own change, on your own transformation. Transform your energy. Transform yourself so that one day, if the people who choose not to change have to endure the negative impact of this choice, you will be there to support them and to teach them that the consequences are the fruit of their resistance and now may be the time for them to change. Or not.

We can never change anyone else.

The only thing we can do is show people love and be a safe haven for those who are going through their own changing process.

JESUS

153

Restriction

I want to talk about loss. All loss. No matter what form it takes.

Every form of restriction functions as a form of loss.

Did you want things to go one way, but they turned out another? Loss.

Did you want things to go faster, but they went slower? Loss.

Did you want something to be bigger, but it was smaller? Loss.

Did you want it to go higher, but it went lower? Loss.

Did you want it to be longer, but it was shorter? Loss.

Did you want love yet received rage? Loss.

Did you want abundance yet received restriction? Loss.

Evidently, whenever the Universe fails to give you what you want, you experience loss.

And what is wrong here?

Is it that the Universe does not give you what you want or that you want so much?

What do you think?

Whenever the Universe fails to answer your wishes, it is because those wishes do not correspond with the existing energy.

You are having difficulty interpreting the signs. You are not receiving the energy that prevails and enables you to navigate.

And why are you failing to see this?

Because your mind is obsessed with what you believe to be correct.

That is the only thing that makes sense to you—what is "logical," as the ego loves to proclaim.

And what if I told you that the world is going through a period of great transformation and that what is right today may not be right tomorrow?

And what if I told you that you need to learn to leave everything in the open so that you can catch the energy of change that is approaching?

What I mean by all this is that whenever you attract restriction, it is a sign that you should go beyond what's "logical" so that you can embrace change.

It sounds difficult, doesn't it?

But I assure you that if you put this concept into practice, you will be one of the pioneers in the times ahead.

And I will be here to guide, inspire, and enlighten you.

JESUS

154

Being Adventurous

I talk to you. I talk to you even if you do not listen, even if you do not recognize my voice. I speak through flowers, fruit, and nature. I speak through the feelings that arise in you whenever you allow yourself the opportunity to contemplate.

And every time I talk to you, I tell you what to do. I tell you what is best for you at an evolutionary and experimental level. At the level of light.

But you do not always hear me. You do not always see the flowers. You do not always contemplate.

You do not always stop to listen to me.

When I speak to you, I give you advice, directions. I show you where your life is headed and where it should be going, where you can be happier and where misfortune lies.

The choice is always yours. I only show you these paths. I do not choose them.

For those who do not listen, there is only loss. Those who do not listen to me cannot correct anything. They must bear the loss and try to learn from it.

The purpose of loss, no matter what form it takes, is to make you realize that you are on the wrong path.

But which is the true path?

Loss is followed by the realization that change is needed. But where do you change? What do you change?

This is the answer that you must strive to discover.

You have an advantage over all those who do not observe the signs. You are aware that you need to change. Others have not yet realized this.

To sum up: you need only discover what it is you must change.

To obtain that answer, look into your heart. Look at your most intimate plans. At what you know you must do, even though you still lack the courage to do so. At what you believe to be illogical, impetuous, and immature.

The more the ego belittles your dream, the stronger and more imperative it will become. Take advantage of your loss.

If what you thought to be good and secure no longer is, if what you thought to be right no longer is, if what you considered to be "normal" didn't work out, be adventurous.

You have already lost.

You have already been denied.

Now take a chance on your most unlikely dream.

Use your loss to go in search of happiness.

JESUS

155

I Want to Talk

I want to keep on talking to you, just as I have always done.

I have always expressed my opinions. I have always communicated. But I communicate in a different way. Not through words but through sensations.

I know it is difficult for you because you are not used to it.

You are used to seeing, listening, touching, speaking, reading.

But feeling? It must seem very strange to you.

Try this. Close your eyes. Breathe. Focus on your breathing and nothing else. Remain like this for a while.

Then make a request. Ask for your ego to be removed. You will feel something enormous taking leave. Then ask for your resistance to be removed. Once again you will feel something enormous taking leave.

Let me warn you that although the ego and resistance leave, it is only temporarily.

Allow a light to enter through your head. Let it run down your body.

Then focus on me. Feel me.

Be aware of my presence.

When you are feeling most at peace, I will be there.

When you feel a great light moving inside you, I will be there.

I will be there in the remoteness of everyday life, in the huge distance that separates this moment of deep emotional response that you are experiencing now, from ordinary life in matter.

And the greater the distance, the greater my presence will be.

And one day, after you have done this exercise many times, you will find me. I will be there, and I will make myself felt.

I am waiting for you.

JESUS

156
Not Having

Let's move on to today's topic.

Today I wish to talk about responsibility.

However, I do not wish to talk about responsibility in terms of what you do, for we have already covered that sufficiently. I do not wish to talk about how you are responsible for what you have and even less about how you are responsible for who you are.

Today, my friend, I wish to talk about being responsible for what you do not have.

Think about what you do not have: what you would like to have today, what you would have liked to have in your life yet do not have.

Acknowledge that there is a reason why you do not have this now.

All matter and all abundance are accessible to you down there on earth.

Everything is at the disposal of your energy. And if you are unable to achieve things, it is simply because those things are not part of your energy.

They are not meant for you because they are not in harmony with the energy you have today.

However, if you change your energy, the things you desire may then become part of your energetic system—not the things you desire in order to become rich, nor those you desire in order to show off to others, only those you want because they bring you happiness when you use them. For in matter, these are the things that will help you become closer to your essence and then to your soul.

And we, up here, never deny a request from the soul when it is energetically appropriate.

To sum up: You are entirely responsible for the things you do not have today. You attracted this situation through the force of vibrating in a certain way. And changing your energetic frequency is about choice and commitment.

Now it is up to you to make your choice and demonstrate your commitment.

JESUS

157
Opportunities

Strictly speaking, all men are equal in the eyes of God.

They all receive the same amount of goodwill, the same amount of tolerance, and the same opportunities.

All of them receive signs. All of them have opportunities for ecstasy, visions, spiritual information, and healing. Each and every one of them. There are no exceptions.

Some of them take advantage of this. They accept it. They commit. They want to evolve, and they place themselves at the service of evolution.

Above all else, they choose the light. With their soul. With their being.

Naturally, these people are much closer to me.

I am not saying they are better or worse, that they are this type of person or that type of person.

I do not pass judgment.

I observe and help.

The saying you use down there, "When the pupil is ready, the master appears," couldn't be closer to the truth.

For those who accept, I help, motivate, and bless.

For those who reject, I become sad but continue to wait.

I know that the day of discernment will come, when they will wake up from centuries of inaction and fear and finally look up at me.

They will finally choose the light.

And I am deeply thankful to these people, for they will help elevate the earth's energy so that others may gain greater awareness. There is nothing I do not forgive them for, for their commitment is honorable and it makes all uncertainty disappear.

JESUS

158

Detachment

You have to let go of all ties.

You should not wait until people die to detach yourself.

Detachment through death is much more painful and cruel.

To detach means not being emotionally dependent.

When you wait for people's death to end your emotional attachment to them, your pain will be significantly greater.

They are no longer there.

You cannot say good-bye.

You can no longer tell them how much you love them.

You can no longer tell them how much you miss them.

When you wait for someone to die so that you can detach yourself from them, you do everything in fits and starts.

There is no serenity, no tranquillity.

There is no peace.

Do not wait for people to die to detach yourself.

Go to them. Tell them how much you love them and how, regardless of that love, you need to go and live your life. You are no longer dependent on them. You do not need them in order to be who you are.

Yet the fact that you become independent does not diminish your love.

It merely diminishes your emotional dependency.

Sometimes the Universe needs to take the people you love away from you in order to induce detachment.

What if you were to it provoke it ahead of time?

JESUS

159

A Closed Door

When a door closes, you will feel that it is closing only if you are standing in front of it. If you are there, leaning against it, refusing to move.

A door closes loudly and provokes loss only among those who do not see any other way.

Those who are up in heaven, elevated . . . those who see things with the distance that heaven encourages, who are aware that bad things happen in order to make you change direction . . . those people do not feel that the door has closed.

They merely feel that this is not the way or that somewhere there is another door they need to look for . . . or that it is not yet time for that door to open and they must simply learn to wait.

Sometimes people become so determined to reopen a door that they fail to see a much bigger gate opening. They look at what is closing and are unable to divert their eyes to what is opening.

Distance. The secret is to gain distance.

Distance, so that you may see the range of opportunities and the impossibilities that exist.

Distance, so that you may see both sides of the situation.

Distance from earth, so you can be up here, closer to me.

JESUS

160

Vulnerability

If you feel sad, be sad.

Make the most of it.

If you feel like crying, cry.

Make the most of it.

It is not every day that you are able to reach that level of vulnerability.

And vulnerability is sublime. It makes you reassess things, relationships.

It makes you question yourself.

It reawakens the flame of extreme sensitivity, the teardrop that is ready to fall from the corner of your eye.

And that sensitivity is your greatest weapon. Through it, you will receive your intuition, your cosmic orders for moving forward.

Without this sensitivity and vulnerability, your life remains on a mental plane and your energetic course is annulled.

This sadness is well received. It is part of the cycle of vulnerability.

And that cycle has to be respected.

There are days you wake up feeling good and other days you wake up feeling awful. This is a dual cycle that alternates and never ends. You work on your sadness, you cry, and you mourn your personal losses so that when the cycle changes and joy emerges, it will be true, great, cleansed, and generous.

Respect these cycles. Respect your sadness just as you respect your joy.

And take note that those who respect the cycles are always welcome in heaven.

JESUS

161

Knowing What Motivates You

What are you committed to?

Who have you made a commitment to?

To your ego, which is able to give you the money and material possessions you value so much?

Is that who you are committed to?

Is that why you run?

Is that what motivates you?

Or is it to your soul?

Is it your soul you live for? Is it your soul you choose at each moment of your life?

Do you choose peace, tranquillity, a feeling that everything is in its place?

You know that no matter how much it hurts or how hard it is, it is for your soul that you accept to live the reality of your days.

It is for your soul that you reject illusion and seek truth.

Always the truth.

Which of them have you made a commitment to?

To your mind, which wants you to believe that everything will work out well as long as you ignore the pain that you feel in your heart every day?

Or to your essence that asks you to cry for the way you hurt today so that tomorrow you may feel truly better . . . truly well?

Which have you made a commitment to?

To your outer self, which craves expensive clothes and cars and desirable houses as well as a stable social status?

Or to your inner self, which wants just love, only love, and nothing more than love?

Upon touching your heart, does the unconditional love I send you from up here leave its stamp on you forever?

Who are you really committed to?

I will never criticize the choice you make, no matter how awful it may seem. I respect your choice. I respect all of your choices, always and forever.

But I want to know.

I simply want to know.

What are you committed to?

JESUS

162
Being Sensitive

I know you are sensitive. You may not know it, but I know you are sensitive.

Your sensitivity is in your pores, your cells, your vibration.

Every time you are hurt, the sky comes crashing down on you.

And you need just to show your sadness, your vulnerability.

As I always say, "Feel the pain so that it may pass swiftly."

Your sensitivity is a four-leaf clover. It is probably your greatest gift, the greatest gift of all.

Being sensitive is more powerful than being intelligent.

Being sensitive is more powerful than being astute.

Being sensitive is more powerful than being rich, pretty, skillful, and friendly.

Being sensitive is more powerful than being strong.

People who are sensitive feel the pains of the world.

Does it hurt? Yes, it does.

But it is a great deal more real, more harmonious, than blocking out your sensitivity and wandering around like a fool under the illusion that everything is going to get better . . . because we know that nothing improves when we do this.

To be sensitive is to have a connection that is complete, direct, uninterrupted, and irreversible.

Is it harder? Yes, it is.

However, when you feel good, when you feel happy—and you will begin to feel this more often—you will feel boundless joy.

What was once joy now becomes ecstasy.

What was once happiness now becomes a state of grace.

And those who are truly sensitive, those who have fully embraced their sensitivity, who no longer block their emotions, who accept everything, absolutely everything, already know what it means to be in a state of grace.

And they no longer want to give this up.

And they no longer desire a different kind of life.

JESUS

163

A Day Just for Me

I would like to see you smile.

I would like you to sing to me.

I would like you to dedicate a day to me only. To hear me, to feel me, especially to feel me.

I would like you to dedicate a day to me, a day free of sadness and lamentations.

A day consisting only of energy. The energy of love. I want you to feel me, calmly and freely, like an allegorical rhythm of light.

You would remain like this, still, simply feeling, and you would slowly begin to let me in.

First I would enter into your heart, and you would immediately begin to feel my love.

Then this energy would begin to enter into every unknown part of your essence, your body, and your energy.

Then your own light would emerge.

After having dedicated some time to me, I would shine even brighter within you.

As this day that you offer me draws to a close, I would slowly begin to leave you. But I would leave you there, still, vibrating for me.

And I, from up above, would be happy for having been able to bring a little more light to earth, through you.

JESUS

164
Quality

What is the nature of your love?
>   Do you love to express what lies deep within your soul?
>   Do you love because you feel?
>   Do you love so as to share what you receive from me?
>   What type of love do you express?
>   Are you able to love and show that you love?
>   Is your heart able to make itself heard?
>   Do those you love feel loved?
>   Are you able to say that you love?
>   Are you able to say how much you love?
>   Or not?

JESUS

165
True Love

When you love someone, you require nothing in return.

True love is felt and bequeathed.

You have no need to receive. Your love does not fade even when you receive the opposite of what you have offered.

True love is when you just simply love.

If you are pleased with what you receive in return, that is wonderful.

But it should not depend on this.

Those who are constantly making demands, who need others to do things in order to be able to love, do not really love.

They have a distorted view of how they would like their love to be.

And they insist on its being this way.

This is not love. It is an illusion.

Those who require others to do certain things, say certain things, and be a certain type of person are just being manipulative.

That is not love. It is control.

Those who truly love feel that their love is unconditional.

Theirs is a pure love, genuine and devoid of "ifs" and "buts."

They simply love.

Just like me.

Just as I love you.

JESUS

166

Being Attentive

I am in the sound a spoon makes when you stir your tea.

I am in nature, in the most basic things.

To pay attention to the smallest details is to pay attention to me.

I know that you want to give me your attention when you meditate, pray, or raise your feelings to heaven. I understand this and am grateful.

But be aware that I am also down there, bestowing light upon the smallest of things, those that you pay no attention to.

You believe I am in the things that are important, and you pay attention only to important things.

And what if I told you that I am in the rain, the flower you stepped on, the animal you failed to take care of, any and every manifestation of life?

And what if I told you that I am in the sound a spoon makes when you stir your tea? That I am in the tea itself and in the solitude of those who stir the tea?

And what if I told you that I am in you, in your heart, inside the most important thing in this world, which you pay no attention to?

And what if I told you that I am in the tears that spring from your eyes when you decide to cry and release all the emotion contained inside?

And what if I told you that I am in that big, wide smile, the honest smile of those who cry when they feel the need to and are joyful throughout the good moments in life?

The next time you do the simplest thing in the world, think of me.

Open your heart, and let me in.

I will be there.

JESUS

167

Making the Most of Things

Have you ever noticed that you sometimes experience things in your life that fill you with joy? They may be unexpected but happy events or long-standing issues that have finally been successfully resolved.

Have you ever noticed how there are times, even if it is only for a brief moment, in which you are extremely happy?

And what do you do with all that happiness? Do you make the most of it? Do you take pleasure in it? Do you take the opportunity to feel, feel, feel, as a way of making up for those days that are not so good and during which you spend your time crying?

What do you do with all that joy?

You immediately run and tell someone about it. You are unable to experience the intensity of it on your own.

And have you ever noticed that the person you share this with never reciprocates this energy?

Have you noticed that since that person is not part of the issue, the most he can do is be happy for you (which may not always happen)?

You continue to share with him, but when he fails to show any enthusiasm, you believe he has a problem, so you confide in someone else, who reacts the same way. And so you begin to wilt, until there comes a point when it is you who are no longer able to feel enthusiasm.

Where did you go wrong?

You drained your energy. You spread it among others. You did not keep it to yourself to fulfill and enlighten you.

If you take a closer look, you will see that you never keep anything to yourself. Then you blame others because they fail to show interest in what you do, for not understanding you.

And since they show no interest, there comes a time when you too stop caring about anything.

You have to learn the following: sometimes there are things we have to keep to ourselves.

You have to treat them like secrets, at least for a while. Keep them to yourself.

Make the most of them, get enthusiastic, and show an interest. And maintain that energy. Sometimes you will feel that you are about to explode. But stay as you are.

This is your energetic sustenance.

This is your sustenance of light.

JESUS

168

Love and Pain

There is a difference between love and vulnerability.

Love is a unique frequency of contentment, entrustment, and endowment.

Love is an act of solidarity from one soul to another.

It is when the heart chakras finally meet and fly toward the great heavens.

It is the highest thing that exists. Love is the highest pattern of vibrational frequency that any human being can desire.

Vulnerability is the opposite of resistance.

To allow yourself to be vulnerable is to choose to switch off. It is to let go of control. It is to accept heaven's directive within your life as well as in your emotions.

To allow yourself to be vulnerable is to let yourself go with the current, without fear or resistance, simply because that is how it should be.

Simply because to let go of all control is, in effect, the only way you allow us to guide your life, to give you sound advice, which is then expressed through your intuition.

I can speak to—allow myself to be heard by—only those who are vulnerable. I can communicate only with those who renounce their ego and do not need to know everything.

I am the one who knows everything.

And why am I sending you a message about the difference between love and vulnerability?

The answer is simple: unless you allow yourself to be vulnerable, you will never love.

If you do not allow yourself to feel the flow of your emotions, if you do not allow yourself to experience pain when it comes, if you do not allow yourself to yield to pain when it comes, then, as I have said before, you will never be able to give yourself over to that emotion that causes the greatest pain.

Love.

And you will be ready to entrust yourself unconditionally to love only when you have acknowledged that you must accept pain when it emerges . . . when you have understood that for things to be good, you must go through moments of pain . . . and when you have completely accepted that everything is duality and that you need to harmonize and accept both sides, each in its own time.

JESUS

169

Two Paths

Taking command of your life. Feeling what needs to be done.

Doing what needs to be done. There are times when life will lead you to a crossroads that is so clear, so evident, that you will have no alternative but to choose.

You may not want to choose.

You may not want to make any decision.

But the day will come when life will take it upon itself to lead you to the perfect crossroads or, to be more precise, to a fork in the road where you must go either one way or the other.

Opposing sides. Opposites. And you will be forced to move.

You cannot remain at a standstill. You cannot move ahead.

There is no road directly ahead.

Either you must turn right or left.

It is at this point that you will have to take command of your life. You will have to focus. You will have to look within.

Do not think.

As often as not, that is what people do when it is time to choose. They think.

No.

This is the time to ascend. To ascend and choose the light.

Every time life leads you to a crossroads or to a place of opposites in which you have to choose, there are normally two options.

One road is light.

The other is almost always density.

I am not saying that one of them is right and the other wrong.

I am not saying that you have to choose the right one.

You may even choose the wrong one.

What matters is that the struggle between light and density become visible so that you may choose.

This is not the time to think. It is not the time to ponder.

It is the time to ascend, to try to feel where the light is, and to follow it.

That is my command.

That is what it means to take command of your life.

Two paths. Having to choose. Accepting to choose the light.

Taking command. Ascending in order to feel which of the roads is light.

Choose. Follow that path.

Good luck.

JESUS

170

The Exact Starting Point

You can discover the meaning of your problems.

Everything that happens to you is speaking to you.

The Universe is constantly talking to you.

Every situation you find yourself in has a meaning.

Every situation you find yourself in had a beginning. A starting point.

A point at which that issue began.

And it is in that moment that you will find the answer.

But that moment may not have been the exact starting point.

When I say the exact starting point, I mean that although you believe that the start of the problem was when it began, this may not be entirely true.

A problem that erupted in your life a week ago may in fact be traced back to the year before, when the foundations were first laid.

And it is at that exact starting point wherein lies the problem.

And the solution.

What type of energy were you emanating at the exact point this problem started? When did it really start?

And when you have answered this question, think about this:

Was the energy you were emanating at that exact starting point the same as the energy emanating from the problem that you are currently attracting?

Calm your heart and ask it:

When did this begin?

When was the exact starting point?

What energy was I emanating at that point in time?

And when you discover the initial energy of that problem—the energy you emanated—in that very moment you may be making history.

In that moment you will have the rare opportunity to change that energy, transforming it into its polar opposite.

Clearly, it is possible to learn from your experiences and change the course of events.

And when that time comes, when you are able to follow this lengthy and painful process, you will have the energy to raise your frequency and never again attract situations with a similar energy.

I guarantee it.

JESUS

171

Perfectionism

Whenever you have a problem, no matter what it is, try to understand what you were emanating at the precise point in which it started. (To learn how to do this, read the previous message.)

When you have understood what you emanated in order to have attracted what you have now, ask yourself the following question:

"Why do I insist on emanating this energetic frequency?

"What am I trying to hide?"

No matter what the answer is, you will find a common denominator in all your answers:

"I want to hide my imperfection."

You want others to see you as perfect so that you will be loved, so that you won't be rejected.

To sum up:

There isn't any type of action, no matter how slight, that will succeed if it is derived from the need for perfection or from a rejection of one's limitations. Problems will arise.

That is why it is so important to recognize the emotion that is behind someone who wants to be perfect.

Because that emotion is called karma.

JESUS

172

Choosing First

People are what they are.

You cannot make them better people, nor can you make them worse.

You cannot do anything for them that they have not chosen originally.

What you can do is help them choose.

And how do you help them choose?

By choosing first.

By making your choice.

By choosing the light and changing your vibrational frequency.

Because when they see you have changed, they will believe that it is possible to change.

And when they realize that it is possible to change, they will begin to look at themselves.

And they will try to change. And this attempt at change is already a change in itself. The fact that they believe it is possible to change is already a huge change.

Do you see why it is so important that you change first?

You could say, "But changing myself is harder."

Of course it is. That is why it is so important.

If there is something you want someone to do, you must do it first.

If there is a certain way in which you want someone to act, you must act that way first.

He may not even do what you want him to, but your transformation has already begun.

And that is what really matters.

JESUS

173

Resistance

Think of a soldier.

Imagine that soldier at war. Think about how he is feeling.

A soldier at war, on the battlefield, having to cope with stray bullets and dead comrades, in what state is his heart?

It is exploding. Exploding with emotion, anxiety, death, torture, and brutality.

The heart of that soldier, who was once a child and believed in life, who once asked JESUS to end all war and for all men to unite and live as brothers. And now he is there, on the opposite side of his dream, in that bloody trench trying to deal with his entire energetic history.

Why do you think this all happens?

Why do you think that a child who once desired peace is placed in a war?

The Universe is perfect, I say.

"How can it be perfect?" you ask.

Think about the fact that man descends to earth to make his light vibrate in density.

Think about the fact that man needs to let go of his resistance so his light can vibrate. Bear in mind that no matter what events we send him, no matter which type of circumstances he attracts, and no matter what sort of life he lives, what really matters is that he give up his resistance.

Regardless of how many warnings we transmit, regardless of how many experiences we send, man insists on remaining strong, standing firm, and holding on to and increasing his resistance.

And the greater number of wars he attracts, the less vulnerable he allows himself to be, the less he yields to the light and to his emotions, and the more he keeps resisting.

Even when he realizes that the harder he resists, the worse things become, he continues to listen to that unrelenting and tiresome voice called the ego.

It would be easier if you were able to understand that if things are not being resolved within this vibrational frequency, it is best to ascend to your own frequency.

It would be easier.

But no, you prefer to believe that you have the answer to everything, and therefore you sink even further.

When are you finally going to understand this?

JESUS

174

Simply Loving

Love. Ah, love. Did you know that more than half of humanity does not open its heart for fear of rejection?

Did you know that more than half of all people wait to be loved so that they can love in return?

Did you know that a great number of people stay with their partners because they feel loved, even though they do not love?

Think about this.

Imagine that one person loves another.

Imagine that the other person does not reciprocate this love. Imagine that instead of continuing to vibrate in that rejection, the first person simply loved. He simply focused on the love he felt. He simply focused on the force of his own vibration without expecting anything in return. What would happen?

What would happen is that this person would not feel rejected, and therefore he would not diminish his own love and live in restriction.

No. He would love.

He would simply love. And that would lift his energy in such a way that eventually he might even end up attracting true love.

JESUS

175

A New Life

A new life beckons you now.

A new life, new people, new events. The past has died. It has to die.

Everything that mattered until now no longer matters; maybe it never mattered. All those theories that appeared viable no longer exist.

You came here to die. To weaken, break, and diminish your resistance.

Nothing has to be perfect. But it has to be new.

New life, new opportunities.

The things that once mattered no longer matter. Now anything that you want to use that belongs to the past—any person, occasion, circumstance, or form of behavior—any fear of feeling will be greatly punished.

The cycle is over.

The flux has ended.

Now I want everything to be new.

Let life present itself, and you will see how wonderful and well organized it is.

JESUS

176

The Best

Bring out what is best in you.

The eyes that express what lies within the soul.

Go and discover.

Allow the goddess (or god) that you are to show itself.

All of you are gods. Why do you try to run away from this?

Why do you try to run, manipulate, lie, seduce, and obtain that which is not yours?

Bring out what is best in you.

You have an essence. You have a light. You have a soul.

By vibrating there, you will shine even brighter.

Go in search of your moon, your unconscious life.

Bring her out into the open, look into her eyes, and let her go.

Only then will I be able to touch your heart. And on feeling my touch, it will react. It will open up, smile, and light up with joy.

But you must be aware and choose what is best in you.

It should be a choice you make on a daily basis, hour by hour, minute by minute, at each and every moment.

At each occurrence, at each rejection, judgment, or feeling of guilt, choose what is best in you.

Cry as much as you need to, but choose yourself.

And you will see how, by doing this, life changes frequency and begins to brighten once more.

JESUS

177

Noncommitment

Vibrate through noncommitment.

You are not committed to anyone or anything.

No one has to be committed to you.

No one has to do anything for you.

Everything people do to you is part of the vibrational frequency that each person has chosen for himself.

People do not do things to you. They do things to themselves.

And you will have to carry only the burden that you are meant to carry.

Imagine that no one owes you anything. There is no "has to."

Imagine that people have their limitations and act accordingly, either remaining in density or choosing the light.

I say remaining in density, because you are already in density. If you stay as you are, you will remain in it.

In order to evolve, you need to change.

Choose the light.

Choose the highest vibration that you are able to reach and stay there.

Remain there.

At each stage a being ascends higher, until there comes a day when he is able to rid himself of misery and comes to vibrate close to my light.

JESUS

178

The Good Side

Today we are going to work on our good side.

The joy of being alive, the joy of being able to choose the best frequency to vibrate in.

Today we are going to rejoice. We are going to celebrate the fact that no matter how dual life is, it has a good side.

Today you need not cry. You do not have to work on your losses, sadness, or weariness.

Today is about honoring communion. The fact that you are part of everything that is life and are able to understand that there are many surprises set aside for you on this journey.

Everything is being carefully prepared. We are joining forces so that all the work you have done will be rewarded.

I am preparing the arrival of a star to guide you more closely.

This is my way of letting you know that you have behaved well.

This is my way of saying thank you.

JESUS

179

Passing Judgment

You know I do not encourage judgment.

You know that to judge is to think you are better than others.

It is to believe that you know everything and others know nothing.

It is to believe that only you have the formula for resolving things and that any effort others make is both futile and irrelevant.

That is what it means to judge.

To judge is to incite division.

Now I wish to talk about analysis.

To analyze is to consider that something is correct or incorrect, according to your own energy.

And this is something I recommend wholeheartedly.

Today there are people who do not analyze anything because they fear they are being judgmental.

They believe that analyzing, trying to work out what is good or bad for them, is itself a form of judgment.

And as a result of having lost the power to analyze, they press on without having the slightest idea of what is happening to them.

To sum up, you should think along the following lines:

If I believe that someone or something is correct in relation to my own energy, I am being analytical.

If I believe that someone "had to do" or "should have done" things differently and that they are "this kind of person" or "that kind of person" for not having done so, I am being judgmental.

As someone down there once said, "I may not agree with what you say, but I will defend to the death your right to say it."

And that makes all the difference.

JESUS

180

Anything Will Do

Anything will do when you need to work on something in your life. When you go to the heart of a problem, to the essence of the emotion those problems cause, it is a way to ease more density and liberate more karma.

You are objects of memory. You are practically absent from the present.

You are 80 percent past and 20 percent fear of reaching into that past, which is why you project everything into the future.

"I am going to do it."

"I am going to succeed."

These are classic statements made by someone who projects all his hopes into the future, not understanding that the future is made up of the choices he makes today.

But to make choices now, you need to be synchronized in the here and now and know how to respond to the impulses the present brings you, as a way to release density.

And only when you release density in the here and now will you be cleansed enough to make choices in the present day that will go on to build a better tomorrow.

As I said, anything will do for you to work on the here and now.

Everything that happens to you, absolutely everything—whether you trip on a stair or a child or parent continuously hassles you—helps to identify what you are feeling.

And in that moment, when you are focused on what you are feeling, look upon that emotion as a memory of a past life in which you found yourself in an identical situation. And call the beam of light to extract that density from your heart.

That is all. That is how it works. Now it is up to you to choose where to use it.

I believe you can always use it, at any time, in any place.

Anytime something or someone bothers you or makes you feel uncomfortable.

That is how it works.

Use it.

JESUS

181

Mother

Sit down. Get in touch with yourself.

Feel each and every one of your veins pulsating. Feel every nerve, every muscle. Feel the sound your heart makes. Feel yourself in the midst of so many involuntary movements.

Now that you have felt your body, feel your soul. Feel its brilliance.

Even if you are unable to see how it shines, believe in the brightness it emanates and never tires of creating.

Now feel the light. That enchanting light that comes from up above, from heaven, and makes everything around you shine.

And this brightness bonds with your soul and we are one.

And for a few moments you are at one with nature, with heaven, with the cosmos.

And for a moment you are God.

And after many years have passed, after many winds have blown, that light will still be there, that intense brightness that keeps humanity awake.

That light, my son, is the mother.

Mother is energy. And if it is energy, it is the greatest of energies.

You will feel that this light guards you, heals you, and keeps you constant company.

This light understands you, feels you, and is easy to deal with. It does not mistreat you. On the contrary, it always brings out the best in you.

This light is your mother. Do not think you are betraying your real mother in this lifetime. No, your mother down there is and will always be your love, your reference on earth, in matter.

However, you need something more.

And today you are going to receive more.

You are going to have your mother in light. From up above, from heaven.

Sit down. Get in touch with yourself.

And allow that light to enter.

You will feel light and cleansed. You will feel that everything is worthwhile. You will understand the reason for your mistakes.

You will understand that heaven is waiting for you when you choose to accept it.

You will understand the new version of time and the new time that comes with choice.

You will feel choice.

And in the end, when you have bathed in your mother's light, when you have felt the eternal forgiveness of all creatures, you will smile. And that smile will be set in heaven awaiting you.

Like a sign.

Like a sign that is waiting for a light.

And that light is you.

JESUS

182

Calmness

There is a calmness.

A calmness felt by those who are righteous. Those who do the things that need to be done.

Those who are where they need to be.

No matter where that place may be.

And that calmness is the greatest living proof that all that happens is meant to happen. But it is more than that.

It also means that you did what you had to do for situations to unfold.

It is the calmness that comes with "At last, the end." It is the calmness of a mission accomplished.

A mission accomplished and an emancipated soul.

JESUS

183

Allowing Yourself to Feel

Allow yourself to just feel. Just as you are feeling now. Respect this.

There are times when you will not want to feel what you are feeling, times when you would prefer to be feeling something else.

"I know that the course of events should not be altered, yet I am feeling the opposite."

What you are feeling is what you should be feeling. Respect and honor this. Honor what you are feeling, for this is your most precious gift.

Everything you have done up until this moment, everything you have experienced up until now, has done nothing other than prepare you for this important truth.

You are what you feel.

You are what you love.

And you may come up against hurricanes, tornados, and wickedness.

But until you accept what you feel, even if it means losing everything, even if it leaves you in the depths of despair . . . until you accept what you feel, you will be unable to be a human being with a defined energetic system. Your energetic system will be vague, slippery, and hostile.

What you feel is your most precious gift. However, for your light to shine you have to accept your feelings and, most important, follow them through.

Acceptance is only part of the process.

And you don't want to leave things unfinished, do you?

JESUS

184

Saying You're Sorry

Do you know what the word "sorry" means?

To be remorseful. "I am full of remorse. Relieve me of this guilt."

What does this mean? It means that people believe they should apologize only when they deliberately do something wrong.

Does this mean you should not apologize when you do something wrong unintentionally?

Does this mean that if you hurt someone you do not have to apologize just because it was not premeditated, because it was not deliberate?

And what about the other person?

The one who was hurt?

Do you not realize that even though it was unintentional, this person was still hurt? That he suffered because of what you did?

Deliberately or not?

We have to take responsibility for all our actions.

And if you did hurt someone, whether it was intentional or not, say you are sorry.

Apologize.

Care for that person.

Obviously, he attracted this. He attracted someone to hurt him in order to process his pain and eventually to unblock it. But that does not absolve you of your responsibility.

The fact that heaven used you as a tool to unblock this person does not mean that you made a conscious or unconscious decision to make him suffer.

No matter what the circumstances, you are responsible for the pain. You should look after him.

"Sorry. I didn't mean to hurt you."

"I didn't know, I didn't realize. I am sorry."

And give him a hug. A hug is a great healer. By doing so you will leave this situation energetically cleansed.

Everyone makes mistakes. That is not the issue. What really matters is how you deal with your mistakes.

And not everyone knows how to say "Sorry."

JESUS

185

Tightness in Your Chest

That tightness in your chest. That is a sign.

You have spent your whole life ignoring it, always moving ahead as if it were of no importance. As if it were not part of you. As if it were not your soul calling out.

Every time you did something to provoke this tightness, every time you decided something, chose something, thought about something that provoked this tightness in your chest, you thought it was odd—but you moved forward.

"Life is to be lived," you thought.

The tightness did not stop, it didn't stop you, and it didn't make you rethink your situation. It didn't make you postpone your journey, at least until you knew what was causing it. No. You tell yourself it will pass. It's anxiety. It's depression. I will take something for it. It will pass.

But the tightness does not disappear. And you get used to living with it, getting along with it.

Until it becomes part of who you are.

You begin to believe it is natural, that this is how one lives and what life is like.

And your soul, which is screaming, calling out for help, calling out for support, can communicate with you only in this way, through a tightness in your chest.

And by neglecting this pain, you are neglecting your soul.

And your soul desperately needs you . . .

It needs your attention, your respect, and your wisdom. It needs your guidance, your guile, and your intelligence, not for you to mistreat it, exclude it, and pretend that it does not exist.

Not for you to reject it, be disrespectful of it or to change it. No.

It needs you to be who you really are, truly and freely.

It needs your wisdom in order to show itself.

And it needs you to choose to reach toward the light.

JESUS

186

Revealing Yourself

Reveal yourself. Reveal yourself. Reveal yourself.

That is all I can say to you.

I can and must tell you to reveal yourself, to reveal what you came here to do, to open your heart and soul.

If people do not understand, then they simply do not understand.

But that is not an excuse for not being who you are and revealing it to the world.

The world exists only so that you may reveal yourself without fear of being rejected.

Without fear of being ridiculed.

How many things do you fail to do because you fear being exposed?

How many experiences have you missed because you feared erring?

Fear of making mistakes stops a person from revealing himself.

And the less he reveals himself, the more he sinks into a well of conformity and monotony.

The day will arrive when this person wakes up and no longer knows who he is because he has been in constant hiding from himself and others. He does not know who he was. And he has no idea who he will become.

Life is made up of experiences. Every time you reject an experience for fear of being exposed, for fear of making mistakes and being judged, every time you give up on yourself because you do not wish to be exposed and judged, you are cheating your soul of experiences. And by cheating it of experiences you are also cheating it of knowledge and wisdom.

Never forget. What matters is not whether you make mistakes.

What matters is not whether you stop making mistakes. The world is dual and imperfect. You are dual and imperfect, and consequently it is more than likely that you will continue to make mistakes regardless of whether or not you reveal yourself.

What matters is how you react to those mistakes, what you learn from them, and how much you evolve from the mistake you have made.

It is a different logic, I am aware of that. But it is the way things are.

JESUS

187

Karma

Think about something you want to do but are unable to.

Or, better still, something that you may not want to do because you know it will cause you great pain.

You may not want to do it but you know you have to do it.

You know this not because of your mind but because of your ego.

You know because of intuition, and this is the greatest form of wisdom that exists.

Think about something you have to do but simply cannot do.

It just doesn't happen. It doesn't work out.

You may even try, but you just cannot do it.

Think about it. Focus on it. Focus only on it.

You will notice something stirring inside your chest. A sense of fear. A feeling of constraint. An uncontrollable urge to flee.

This is probably your biggest knot.

Your biggest difficulty.

One of your karmas. Karma is something that caused you a lot of pain in another lifetime. It is blocked, and it is something you are running away from with all your strength in this lifetime.

You have a memory of that life in which it caused you so much pain. An unconscious memory, yet it is still a memory.

And that memory prevents you from doing something similar in this lifetime.

And you may ask, "If I cannot do it, why is it that I want to do it? Why do I know that I have to go there?"

And I will answer: Because this karma has to be unblocked within this lifetime.

And if you come into this life to cleanse karma, until you have relived this memory and accepted the pain, you will be unable to free that karmic energy. So you will be doing nothing worthwhile here.

In short:

Identify the thing that you have most difficulty doing, or even think about doing it. Let your fear take hold of your heart, open your heart, remove that density, cry if you feel the need to, but cleanse yourself.

And each time you think about it, it will hurt a little less.

This is how one begins to cleanse karma. This is how one begins to give meaning to reincarnation.

JESUS

188
Appearances

Think about something in your life you have resolved.

It wasn't easy to resolve, but it has been sorted out.

It took a while, it was hard, but you did it, didn't you?

Think about something that seems to have been resolved.

Really think about it. Just let your imagination flow.

And now begin to dismantle this image.

Dismantle any picture that comes into your mind. Remove the layers of matter and the layers of protection that exist.

And when you have removed everything, you will be left with just one emotion.

Allow that emotion to grow inside your chest. Allow it to grow inside your chest, regardless of how strange it may seem. Let it take over. Begin to respect this emotion even if it seems contradictory, even if you do not understand it.

Emotion is the bearer of all wisdom. Simply accept it regardless of which emotion it may be.

And you will see that the situation is not as well resolved as you thought it was.

JESUS

189
Hero

Who is your hero? What is he like? What qualities does he have?

What do you admire in him? What qualities do you see in yourself?

"I would really like to be like him, to have what he has, to do the things he does."

Have you ever caught yourself thinking this?

Do you know what it means?

It means you want to be or have or do things that are not meant for you, at least not at this moment.

It means you waste so much time focusing your attention on someone else and the things this person has that there is no room left for you to concentrate on what's best in you.

I am not saying that you will never be, have, or do what that person is, has, or does. That is not what I mean.

What I am trying to say is that whatever it is that you want to be, have, or do, it will have to be based on who you already are, what you already have, and what you already do. This is the starting point. It is from this point that you will expand your dynamics.

It is you who expands on what already exists, not someone else who exists and then passes his gifts on to you.

For when you focus too much on who a person is, what he has and what he does, your focus is limited. You do not see the person as a whole. It is as if he had only good qualities and no flaws at all. Therefore, by wanting to be like that person, what you are saying deep down is that you do not want to have flaws. And this is not possible.

You can have heroes, you can wish to be like someone you admire, but you have to recognize that it all begins from within you. You may expand on what you have. You may even begin to be or have new things.

But you can never be someone else.

Simply because no two energies are alike.

JESUS

190

Meditation

Do this exercise.

Close your eyes, breathe.

Breathe deeply.

Allow a light to enter through your head. Even if you cannot see it, feel it.

Feel my light entering and moving through your whole body.

Then focus on the people you care about.

Imagine that they are inside your energy. You brought them inside because you love them so much.

And now, one by one, remove them from your energy.

It doesn't matter how long it takes you to do this exercise.

Remove them from your energy, one by one.

Ask each of your cells to open up, so as to expel the energy of these people from your energetic system.

You are not sending them out of your life. You are only sending them out of your energetic system. When you have finished, breathe in once more. Deeply. And once again allow my light to enter through your head and move along your entire body.

Now let's move on to your work or study, whatever it is you do for several hours a day, every day.

You are going to remove this energy from within you.

No matter how long it takes, work on removing the energy of your daily chores from your energetic system, cell by cell.

Then money. Focus on that energy. Remove it. Let go of that energy from inside your body.

Don't get agitated. You are not removing money from your life, but rather its energy, which is dense and arrogant.

Breathe. Receive light through your head. Now your emotional relationships, love or the lack of it.

Remove that energy. Allow each cell to expel that energetic force.

Now for health or the lack of it. Each cell will expel the energy belonging to health.

Now for the people you do not like or do not get along with. Feel their energy. Remove it from within each cell.

And last of all, your problems. Remove them, let go of the energy of your problems, and, even more, let go of all the energy that does not belong to you.

And continue to receive my light, down through your head.

And focus on releasing the energy that is not yours. Every cell will become less occupied so as to allow my light to enter.

Feel my light.

Ask me to enter.

And I will step inside you. And we will stay together in light until the world shakes us awake.

JESUS

191

Rage

What is rage?

Rage, I always say, is the "air bag" of sadness.

What do I mean by this?

What I mean is that when you get mad at someone, when you get mad at something, it is because you are sad.

And your sadness hurts. It hurts a lot. So your ego reaches the conclusion: "Why do I have to go through this pain? Because someone has done something to me."

And you find someone to blame. And immediately you stop focusing on yourself and begin to focus on someone else, the "guilty person."

After continuously judging him, you begin to feel rage.

I have something to tell you.

Rage feeds off itself. The more rage you feel, the more rage you will feel. And sooner or later you will fall ill.

You will fall ill because you are constantly angry, because that poison inside you, that extremely low frequency, will end up seeping through your cells and killing them.

Is that what you want?

The only solution is to transform that rage into sadness.

Are you full of rage? Stop.

And think.

Are you sad? Why?

Stay as you are feeling. Sad.

Stay as you are. Stay just as you are. Cry if you feel the need to.

Focus on your sadness and not on who supposedly hurt you.

Who knows if you attracted this—if the Universe sent you this person—to harm you, to provoke your sadness, so that on feeling sad you could look within yourself and find a beautiful, sensitive, and highly energetic person?

Who knows?

Until you feel sadness, you will not be able to look within yourself and feel how pure your soul is.

If you continue to feel rage, you will not concentrate on yourself, you will focus only on those who are supposedly guilty, and you will never look inside yourself.

Think about this.

Isn't the Universe perfect?

I think so.

JESUS

192

Questions

Even if you cannot see me, you can ask questions.

Even if you cannot hear me, you can ask questions.

Even if you cannot feel my light, you can ask questions.

And the secret is nothingness. In going to zero, in remaining empty. In how much ego and resistance you can remove. In how many thoughts and how much mental density you can remove.

The secret is in the ability to be intuitive but, more important, to believe in intuition. The secret is in the ability not only to feel but, more important, to believe in what you feel.

Do the following.

Have you got a question?

Good. We will give you an answer.

Do the following.

Sit comfortably. Breathe.

Start placing your thoughts on a shelf, which you will find hanging in heaven.

Become an observer of your own thoughts. But do not criticize.

Do not express an opinion.

Another great secret to coming to heaven is having no opinion.

The fewer opinions you have, the more open you will be to what I have to show you.

Now allow a light to enter through your head.

Even if you cannot see it, allow it to enter.

This light is going to run through your whole body, and you will feel lighter.

Then, and only then, ask your question.

Do not think about the answer. Do not think about the answer, even for a second.

Just wait. Ask the question and wait.

Wait without forming an opinion, without thinking about it.

Do not forget that you are merely an observer.

Soon you will begin to feel something.

Remain just as you are. Do not think. Do not begin to form an opinion.

Just continue to be an observer of events.

At zero. Completely empty.

And the answer will begin to unfold before you.

It may be an image, it may be an emotion, but whatever appears will be full of meaning.

And if you are able to stay at zero, without criticizing, without judging, without wanting anything, absolutely nothing, other than the truth from up here, from heaven, the answer to your questions will begin to appear, and it will be strong, loud, and clear so as to do away with your uncertainties.

You may not like the answer. You may feel sad, or you may vibrate through happiness.

But this is the truth I have for you, and at least you have the consolation of knowing you no longer have to vibrate in illusion.

And this in itself is already a great achievement.

JESUS

193

Reverence

Revere the light. Let it know how much you love it, how much you identify with it, how special you know it is.

It is the star that lights up your life, the ship that navigates you beyond the horizon, taking you to ancestral dimensions so that you may rescue the lost pieces of your soul.

Show reverence, acknowledge how magnanimous and strong the light is, how supreme it is, how it has become the master of your energy.

And follow it. Follow it to the end of the world, if need be, so that you may rescue what is most pure in you, discover what is most original in you, and add color to your life.

To give flavor to your existence, to give meaning to it, yield to the light.

Yield and recognize that there is no other way of living in communion.

Show reverence.

There is no other way to evolve than this.

Show reverence.

Make a commitment.

And resolve that from now on, you will never deceive yourself again, lie to yourself, or delude yourself.

Not even to escape from pain.

Never again.

JESUS

194

Edification

Everything up here is to be made known down there.

Everything you see up here is to be completed down there.

Everything you feel, everything you perceive is aimed at helping you to be edified.

Man feels, perceives, and goes to earth to be edified.

This is the process. There is no other.

Down there, you may want to do what makes you feel more at ease, what is less complicated for you.

You may even mislead yourself into believing that there are things you must do that are taxing yet essential, given that you are doing them for others . . .

Or because you are doing them for me.

I do not need you to do anything.

I am fine.

But you are not.

You have to come up here, abandon your ego, and begin to receive information, receive instructions concerning what you should or should not do.

Not what you must do but rather what you should do, for we only suggest. The final choice is always yours.

And once you understand and accept that the things you want may not always be suitable for your journey (though the things up here are meant for you and will almost certainly be so) . . .

When you realize that there are things you feel deep down that you have to do, even if you do not know why, and you do them . . .

At that point, you will be an initiated soul, and your life will radically change.

At that point, you will have the strength that comes from the soul, and everything will become easy, clear, and cleansed.

At that point, you will have moved closer to me.

JESUS

195

You Deserve It

Imagine that life is waiting for you. Imagine that the life you never dared dream of, a life filled with music and song, is ready to devote itself to you in all its magnitude.

Imagine that there is a life where you are happy, where everything that surrounds you is in accordance with your energy, discreet and subtle.

Imagine a life where you could be, feel, talk, and live, and where all those around you would understand your roots, your motives, and your logic.

Imagine that the life that is available to you is far-reaching and may truly elevate you.

And that the concessions you must make—because down there, in the dual world, there is always a need for concessions—would be minimal, secure, and peaceful.

That life exists.

It exists, and it is ready for you. It is ready to introduce itself.

But you have to make a choice.

You have to choose to deserve it.

To deserve happiness, to deserve to live without guilt, to deserve kindness, understanding, and affection. To be worthy of love.

And most of all, to be worthy of unconditional love.

Mine.

From up here.

And when you have chosen all this, you will rid yourself of your old habits, you will rid yourself of your emotional dependencies, you will rid yourself of endless concessions, and you will look within yourself.

And you will see your essence glowing.

And you will see that it also deserves a chance.

And you will look for it before you look for anything else.

It will become the guiding star of your life.

And you will look at others no longer as emotional crutches but as fellow travelers on your journey.

Whom you demand nothing from.

To whom you give the unconditional love you come up here to get.

And so, feeling light and fluid, you will begin to fly through life in search of your own life.

And your life will have room to reveal itself.

And you will have the opportunity to embrace it.

And together you will travel the heavens toward eternity.

JESUS

196

Seeking Love

This is the thought I want you to ponder:

Human beings do not come to earth to get love.

They come to earth to give love.

The love they come up here in search of.

Think about it.

Human beings have been coming to earth without any connection, spirituality, or ties.

And as human beings need love, there is a natural tendency for them to try to find love down there on earth.

It just so happens that there are other human beings also looking to meet their own needs.

And so people cross one another's paths through neediness.

They need one another. They need understanding, love, and affection. And they look for them in others.

Of course, that can never work.

Rarely do our needs coincide with what others have to offer.

That is not the logic by which things work. In truth, humans should not look for those feelings in others.

It hardly ever works out.

Because then they start to demand things in return.

You just have to look at couples to see this. What do they complain about?

More often than not their complaints are based on expectations that have not been met. "I want him to be this type of person, and he isn't." "I want him to do this, but he doesn't."

Each one demands what he wants from the other and is unable to respect that person for who he truly is.

What is the outcome?

Needy lives in which people try to get their partners to fill their emotional void.

What is the solution?

The only viable solution is for human beings to start looking up to heaven.

To meet their needs up here.

They can come here for understanding, protection, support, kindness, playfulness, affection, commitment, security, and spiritual comfort.

But above all, they can come here for unconditional love.

That sentiment in which you are loved for who you are, without restrictions or reservations, together with all your flaws and qualities, together with your vulnerability and fearlessness.

I am the one who loves you.

And you are going to keep this love inside your heart in such a way that you will then feel the need to distribute it throughout the world to the souls who cross your path.

And in this way, you will have fulfilled one of the greatest missions man has on earth:

To take love to earth rather than to take love from earth.

Think about this, come up here, and see how different everything can be.

From the moment you look at me.

JESUS

197

Wings

Lift your wings so that you may fly. Care for your wings with affection, diligence, and determination.

With affection so that they may grow freely and unburdened.

With thoroughness so that heaven will always appear to you as the great and respectful creator of the stars.

And with determination so that you will never give up, even when your wings are a long way from flying, a long way from heaven, and a long way from the light.

"How should I tend to my wings?" you ask.

It is simple, my friend, as all things are up here in heaven.

Elevate yourself.

Increase your vibration. Take care that all your thoughts, actions, and worries always, and on every occasion, reflect the highest energetic pattern that you are able to conceive.

Take care that your ego, judgment, guilt, and resistance always stay light-years away from your energy.

Take care that you cherish your dreams even when you are unable to make them come true.

An unfulfilled dream is still a dream.

Or it may transform into frustration.

The choice is yours.

And most important, take care that when you come up to heaven you lift your wings as high and as far as your energy can reach.

And soar above the heavens with the strength of my protection.

And when you return to earth, when you return to your everyday life, you will feel this higher realm inside your body.

And if you close your eyes and breathe, you will still be able to feel the movement of the wings upon your back.

And no one will know what took place.

And no one will know that you can fly and that you have powerful wings.

And no one will know how happy you are.

It will be a secret.

Yours and mine.

Yours, mine, and of the whole universe.

And when someone tries to clip your wings, you will realize that there are concessions you never make.

And this is one of them.

JESUS

198

Life Introducing Itself

Your life has strength. It has energy.

It has a will all its own.

If you stopped doing all the things you do today, if you stopped worrying, if you stopped rationalizing and being controlling, you would notice something phenomenal.

A phenomenon that few people witness, precisely because they are unable to stop doing the things they do, unable to stop worrying, rationalizing, and trying to be in control.

And if you can do this, you will finally be able to see life introducing itself.

You will realize that life moves on its own. It moves forward by itself.

Life moves on its own accord, filled with energetic gravity.

You will be only where you need to be.

You will do only what you need to do.

This is an unbending universal law.

And everything that contradicts this will only attract pain, loss, and suffering.

And who knows where you should be now and what you should be doing now?

Who? you ask.

You? Your ego?

No. Life.

Only life knows where to go, which way to go, and how to get there. Only life.

And if you stop thinking that you know, that you can, and that you have to, you will allow life to carry you.

You will put life first.

You will recognize that it is right.

And life—light and free; such is its nature—will meet the demands of your journey and lead you to success.

And everything will be in its rightful place. And at the end, we will meet up here to commemorate your life.

JESUS

199
Faith

Faith opens the channel.

Think about this sentence. Think about what it means, what it is trying to say.

The fact that you believe in what you see, what you hear, and above all in what you feel . . . the fact that you understand how sensitive communication with heaven is and you devote yourself to exploring this connection . . . the fact that you realize that the act of believing is itself subtle and brave, all this leads to your channel opening up immensely.

And the more this channel opens, the more intuitive you become and the more you believe . . . and the more the channel opens.

This is the cycle. This is the path.

In truth you have only two alternatives.

To choose to believe in what you feel, in your intuition, and, in doing so, open the doors to a wonderful and authentic way of being in life.

Or to fill yourself with doubt, stop believing, allow your ego to enter, and live a life full of frustration and pain.

As always, the choice is yours.

The only thing I can say is that if you believe, even if you do not understand, even if things are not very clear, you will be opening the door to faith, beginning a long and imperceptible journey that will take you to the richest realms of your soul.

And subsequently, to the fullest realms of energy in which you are able to vibrate.

There are no words to describe this state.

It is outside the domain of speech.

It has entered the domain of God.

JESUS

200

Magnet

First, analyze what you attract.

I have spoken about this subject in great depth in my communication.

It is simple.

You attract everything that happens to you—objects, people, circumstances and events.

Inside your chest there is a diamond that is like a magnificent magnet.

This magnet communicates with the Universe and it attracts situations with the same vibrational frequency.

If there is violence in that diamond, you will attract violence.

If there is compassion in it, you will attract compassion.

Everything on the outside mirrors what is inside.

And you have to choose from inside what you wish to manifest on the outside.

If you are able to grasp this very simple yet very accurate rule, you will realize that it is possible to change life through choice, by using your free will.

In short:

Choose to change what is inside. Stop looking outward.

As the saying goes, "Change—and the world changes with you."

JESUS

201

Deciphering

To begin with, analyze what you have.

I explained this in the previous message. You may read it.

But now I wish to talk about something else.

Imagine that you already have the ability to analyze what you attract. That by now you are capable of carrying out this procedure as well as changing what is inside your heart in order to alter what comes out.

Imagine that you already do all this.

Now I want to move on to something else.

Nowadays, what are you working toward?

To have the things you love?

Or to love what you have?

Pay attention:

Most people try to have and possess the things they love.

These may be objects, which we label consumerism.

"I love something so I want it!"

They may be people, and this we label possessiveness.

"I love that person and want him or her all to myself!"

However, as you may have realized, this is not the best way to go about things.

First, this type of behavior does not allow you to move away from the material dimension.

Second, since it is the ego that desires, fighting for what you want is not an attitude that belongs to the soul.

So which standpoint should you take?

I am going to teach you one of heaven's best-kept secrets.

Come up here.

Ask me or your Higher Self what we have in store for you, what is intended for you in this incarnation.

And you will receive a sensation, an image, energy.

And you will understand that it is meant for you down there.

Many of those who try to do this stop here. Why?

Because they do not understand, and thus they do not believe.

Have you ever thought that you may come to understand what we have for you only farther down the line?

Have you ever thought that what we give you is an enigma that needs to be deciphered, but since most people do not know this, they simply discard it?

Be aware of the following:

What we have for you at this moment is what is best and most compatible with your energy.

But you need to decipher it.

It may last only a day . . . or it may last a lifetime. There is no time or space here.

But you have to decipher it. You have to believe that it is really meant for you, and you have to make sense of it.

The energy of what we have for you is not visible, just as your soul's energy is not visible.

It is secret. It is a secret.

You have to continue deciphering. Bit by bit. And as you decipher, you will find many more answers. And you will open up.

And the more you decipher and the farther you open up, the more compatible these energies will show themselves to be.

Something that would never be revealed in the mental dimension.

So you have to continue deciphering.

But not everyone is ready for this. Only a few have the gift of faith and being able to decipher.

And you are one of them.

JESUS

202

Life in Light

Come up here.

To see what you can do, down there.

To doubt. To be afraid.

Work on your fear.

Implement this down there.

With thoroughness. By making adjustments. Without outbursts of ego, without complacency.

Just be thorough. Make a commitment to implement what exists up here in light.

That is all.

And this is what life should be about. Life should be about only this. To come up here and to then put it all into practice down there.

Use your intelligence, use the mental dimension to organize strategies and reunite armies so as to implement the life in light that you have up here, down there.

That is all.

And why does this prove to be so complicated?

Because of fear.

Because of control.

Can you do it?

JESUS

203

A Twist of Your Wings

It seems that people want to do only what they are familiar with.

What they know gives them comfort.

Naturally, there is never any risk for those who think this way.

There is never an element of surprise.

They surround themselves with their own concepts, which are often based on preconceptions, as a way of avoiding risks and "committing" an adventure.

I say "committing" because it would seem that to venture out is a crime.

To take a risk, to go in search of the unknown.

To add an element of surprise.

Yes indeed, the element of surprise.

Imagine that a bird is flying, yet with a twist of its wings in midflight it changes direction abruptly, without prior warning, without preparation.

At the calling of the wind. At the calling of life.

Go on, take a risk. "Commit" your element of surprise. Agree to follow those unknown paths.

Move out of your comfort zone.

Take a risk.

Only the great adventurers have a crystal-clear essence.

Only the great adventurers have great stories to tell.

JESUS

204

Emotional Heritage

Think about what it means to be in the here and now. Focused on the here and now. In this precise moment. Where you are physically rather than where your mind allows you to be.

Each moment is precious, a gift in itself.

Each moment is precise in its intention.

Each minute you are alive is a time for experiences, for choices and reflection.

You live what you have to live in the present moment. You choose what is best for you and, from then on, live this experience.

And the result of the choice you have made will be your future.

In short, the choices you make today will be reflected in the future.

And when the future arrives, you will realize that it was worth staying in the present.

It will be a more fitting future. It will be a more blessed future.

Live each and every minute. Each moment.

Learn to store away positive emotions.

Every sunset, every breathtaking vision, every moment spent with your loved one, every minute you are alive.

Enjoy and hold on to them. Enjoy and hold on to them.

This will be your emotional heritage. A heritage that will always be on hand when you are feeling sad, when you are feeling downcast.

Each minute of ecstasy that you live in life should be kept for all eternity.

It should be stored away for the future.

You may need it.

JESUS

205
Questioning Yourself

These are times of deconstruction.

Everything they taught you to take for granted no longer is.

Or may no longer be.

Or at the very least should be questioned.

Everything you believed to be certain may fall apart at the seams.

Things are not the problem. You are the problem.

You may try to get things to turn out well, the way you always imagined they would.

You may do your utmost for things to remain as they are so as to avoid feeling scared and uncomfortable.

You may try.

But you will not succeed.

All the old structures are now falling apart.

Everything you counted on, you may now discard. You may stop counting on them.

Question them.

Question everything.

Even if you find it hard. Even if it means you have to let go of control.

What is here today may not be here tomorrow. Or may never again exist.

Question everything. Work, relationships, family, finances, security, protection, everything.

And if you think this is still not enough, do something that is even more radical:

Question yourself.

Call into question your position at work. Question yourself in terms of your relationships, your family, and your finances.

Question yourself, and you will see a new "I" emerging.

One who is more secure, more adventurous, and stronger overall.

Not with the strength that stems from the ego but with the strength of someone who has accepted that everything may change and anything may happen as long as you do not renounce that pure and crystalline energy that makes up the being you are.

JESUS

206

A Paradigm or Different Angle

Change. I am always talking about change. A change of path, a change of life. A change of structure and a change of view.

The more you change, the more your outlook will open up to infinity, to new dimensions.

We up above are not particularly worried about the change that is taking place down there, the change in matter itself.

You may change wife, husband, job, or even country.

But that will get you nowhere if you do not change who you are as a person.

There are people who spend their whole life changing in matter, and they remain the same person throughout all that time.

This has gotten them nowhere in terms of evolution.

Now, imagine someone who doesn't change for thirty, maybe forty years and remains in the same job and the same marriage for the same number of years, yet is able to be different each and every day, having the capacity to reinvent himself. He is able to experience every aspect of life down there. It would seem that this person has not changed at all. But that does not hold true for us up above.

We are interested only in the inside. What is inside you.

Therefore, before thinking about making great changes in matter, which may end as great catastrophes, think about just changing your patterns. Change your line of vision, and look upon the old and onerous as inspiration to go further, be more open and free.

Take a look at yourself. See your relationships to things. How you see them.

Think about observing them from way up here, from a purer, more ancestral angle.

You will feel the gratitude from those who inhabit heaven entering you.

The gratitude we feel every time one of you opens up your inspiration to the light is commonly known as unconditional love.

Feel that love. Feel it. Look at all your problems through the paradigm of that love.

And you need not change anything, for life will change for you.

JESUS

207

Reinventing Yourself

Reinvent yourself.

Look at your highest self and reinvent yourself.

Be more audacious.

Be more vigorous.

Be more energetic.

Be freer.

Be more caring.

Be more essential.

Never abstain from who you are when you are in the highest vibration that you can conceive.

Always continue to pursue the creativity you need to reinvent yourself.

Always. Always. Always.

Consistency is for the poor of spirit.

JESUS

208
Butterfly

The butterfly flies.

It simply flies. Comes to rest, stays for a while, then flies again.

Without attaching itself to anything or anyone. Its only concern is to make the forest more beautiful.

It carries everything and everyone in its butterfly heart, and nothing more.

It does not depend on them.

It does not depend on their love or their presence.

It only loves. It loves and flies. It loves and flies.

Be like a butterfly.

Do not become attached to anything or anyone.

Keep everything inside your heart.

Love and fly. And make the forest a more beautiful place.

JESUS

209
Filter

"Nothing is true or false, everything is the
color of the crystal you look through."
AUTHOR UNKNOWN

You see things in relation to your fear.

You look at life, people—in short, at everything—in relation to your own survival.

Let me explain more clearly.

If there is something you are scared of, for example, it is only natural that you protect yourself from it. That you set up defenses. That you create what I call, "layers of survival."

Layers of survival are defenses you create in order to avoid fear and ultimately as a way of avoiding pain. And this may be pain that was never healed in past lives. This is exactly what these layers are. Layers. And you continue putting on layers of defenses, one by one.

Year after year, life after life, you create strategies so that the pain stays where it is, shut down forever.

That's what you hope for.

The truth is that these layers of survival are rather similar to a distorted filter through which you can no longer see reality. You see only an illusion of reality, and this illusion is created by this filter.

When two people with different layers of survival look at the same reality, their filters reflect different experiences.

This gives rise to different opinions about the same thing.

The fact that two people have a difference of opinion is not a bad thing. Truth be told, it is neither good nor bad. It is what it is.

The problem arises when both of these people want to be right. They want their vision to be the real one, the right one.

They do not take these filters into consideration.

They do not take fear into consideration.

They do not take memory into consideration.

They do not take reality into consideration.

JESUS

210

Dawn

Picture yourself like the dawn. What is dawn? It is the birth of a new day.

And with a new day comes so much wisdom.

The wisdom of days gone by, which contains experience acquired through the passage of time and the wisdom of being at zero with a whole new day ahead of you.

Zero in the sense of knowing that what is on its way is new, different, and unfamiliar. And sometimes even incomprehensible.

But the day knows that what is on its way is meant for it. For some known or even unknown reason, everything that arrives is intended for this day.

So that it may feel, understand, assimilate, and evolve.

And always, always cleanse.

Cleanse the things that do not belong to this day but that came and remained. Cleanse what is part of this day, the old density acquired because cleansing was put off for so long. Cleanse what belongs to it and is recent, and bring things up to date.

Be like the dawn.

With dawn comes the wisdom of the past and the ignorance of the future.

And it is here. Ready to begin.

Despite the storms. Despite the distressful days. Despite the rain, the cold, and the sadness.

The dawn knows that it must advance. Daybreak is about to take place, and there is nothing that can stop the sun from rising, even when clouds loom.

Be like the dawn.

Let your past instruct you, but do not allow it to hold up the present and even less so the future.

Be open to what you do not yet know. Keep yourself intact for what is yet to arrive.

JESUS

211

Inner House

I read your thoughts. I know that far more often than not, you are unhappy, tormented by the notion that each person should value his or her essence, and that you do not have the time to do this.

Rarely can you find time for yourself, and when you do, you are seldom able to take advantage of it.

There are too many expectations and too much anxiety and guilt.

"I should be doing something else. There are so many important things to do," you think in anguish.

You fail to understand that your essence regards the short time you have for yourself as precious.

It is time to go to your winter garden, sift through all the emotional information that is there, and feel it, feel it, feel it.

Since you are unable to carry out this process of spending time with yourself, life comes along and pushes you into a bottomless pit where only solitude and darkness lie.

I know. I also read this in your thoughts.

Well, the only thing that I can say to you at this point is: Begin to clean up that darkened space. Begin to clear the dust out.

That is your deepest dwelling, it is your trademark, and it is your daytime abode.

Is it dark? Yes.

Is it dirty? Yes.

Centuries and centuries of abandonment. The trees are desiccated, and the vegetable garden has died.

You will have to replant everything.

You will have to prune, water, fertilize, and love.

You will have to cleanse everything with your pain.

It will move you. You will feel emotional. You will become aware of who you are. And I promise you that you will see yourself again.

You will breathe life into your own foundation. You will use your own bread to nourish yourself.

You will elucidate and transcend yourself.

You will become enlightened.

And when all this work is complete, when all the ghosts have been removed, you will know that you have succeeded.

You will look up and let out a shout of gratitude that will echo throughout space.

And you will see me.

And you will feel me.

And you will know just how much I love you.

And you will have a precise notion of just how great communion is.

And you will know you are healed.

JESUS

212

Changing Vibration

Think of animals. Have you ever noticed that they are normally the color of their surroundings?

Have you noticed that insect wings are the color required for them to blend into their background?

That a fish is the color of the ocean it inhabits?

Now think in terms of frequency.

Think that, just like animals, you human beings should live in an environment that matches your vibrational frequency.

Someone who has too much inner violence will end up attracting a violent environment.

This is the law of nature. This is the law of energy.

Nevertheless, in the midst of all this, there is some good news.

And the good news is that one of the main advantages that human beings have over animals is that they can choose and change their vibrational frequency and consequently change the environment that surrounds them.

And how can you go about changing this vibrational frequency?

Gratitude.

The secret is gratitude.

You can vibrate through gratitude. Feel gratitude for all that you have, for all that life has given you.

If you do not think this is much, feel grateful for what you are already able to feel. For the path you have traveled. For the awareness you have gained.

And last, feel gratitude for me. For having already found me.

For our knowing each other. And for my having spoken to you, even if there are times you cannot hear me.

Find a reason—there are always reasons—and feel grateful.

And you will see how this feeling will begin to grow in your chest. You will begin to emanate gratitude, you will begin to vibrate, the relationships you have with others will change, you will begin to receive more, and you will feel even more grateful.

More and more. More and more.

And the world will change. It will change because something in your vibration has changed.

And around you, everything will become brighter, miraculously.

And the gratitude you feel as a result of the world changing will be so great that it will change the vibration of your home, your road, your city and your life.

And things will never be the same again.

I will have raised my vibration even higher.

And when you leave that plane, once together in heaven, we will talk about your foolishness on earth and how you were brave enough to finally actively embrace your evolution.

JESUS

213

The Honesty of the Essence

I have something to tell you.

Imagine that you are in a room.

Picture yourself motionless in this room.

Look at how you had to protect yourself, how you had to reduce everything around you to its essence in order to reduce your own essence.

Notice how the more you have, the more you can cover up your essence and prevent it from shining.

An essence that shines is a happy essence.

Every time you are able to vibrate through the purest harmony of your essence, the more success you will have in raising your vibration and reaching the heavens.

"And how do you vibrate through your essence?" you ask.

It is easy.

Sit down. Calm yourself. Meditate. Ask to be given the energy of absolute honesty, which is part of your essence.

Ask for the energy of honesty to come inside you.

Keep it there. Stay in that energy as long as you can.

Feel honesty.

Honesty within your being. Honesty within your essence.

Truly feel your essence.

And then ask, in all honesty, to see what in your present life is not honestly in accordance with your essence.

But be prepared for what follows, for it may be the very thing that you imagined would always be part of your life.

And you will have to face this with honesty.

In spite of how much it hurts, you should ban this from your life, simply because it does not belong to you. It does not have your energy, and therefore it only holds you up.

"But why is it the very thing I always thought would be part of my life?" you ask.

"Why does it seem to be so right for me yet, by the looks of it, is so completely unsuitable for me?"

Because you are so withdrawn from your essence's vibration that you have confused it for another vibration.

In reality, you are vibrating there and not here, in your center.

That is why you believe that whatever appears to you will have your vibration.

But no. You are in another vibration.

In this meditation, ask for the honesty of your essence. Ask to know what carries a different vibration in your life and ban whatever it is from your life.

I have spoken.

If you wish to understand this and do what I say, fine.

If you do not wish to understand and are not interested in making energetic and evolutional changes in your life, that is also fine. I will always be here for you.

I never get angry. I never get upset. I never worry. I am not in a hurry. I have time.

I will always be here when you need me. I will always be here when you want to begin. I will always be here when you want to return home.

JESUS

214
Creativity

Life is an adventure. And this is the way it should be lived.

Never repeat the same experiences. Always be innovative, always be innovative.

Consider that beings come to earth to experience emotions.

And to help them with this task, we created experiences in matter.

Experiences in matter create emotion, and beings experience this emotion.

It is a closed circuit that functions incredibly well.

Now imagine the people who never create new experiences in their lives: the kind of people who always do the same things, day after day, year after year, because they think change is bad. They do not venture out, they do not take risks, and they do not throw themselves off a cliff's edge without first knowing exactly what is waiting for them below.

It never even crosses their mind that I could be down there, waiting.

And that I may send a vessel to steer them to heaven.

They have no faith. They do not commune.

These people do not experience life in its entire dimension.

They never step out of their comfort zone. They do not take risks. They do not lose, but neither do they gain anything.

And so life becomes predictable. And it starts to become boring.

And one day they realize that nothing interests them anymore.

This is the day their essence dies.

It is the day that experience in matter ends because of the lack of raw material.

Because of the lack of experiences.

Everything becomes repetitive.

Everything becomes insipid.

Everything loses its form.

And this is not what life is about.

Life is a great adventure.

With new experiences to be lived.

New. All new.

Work on making your life less repetitive.

Create situations. Create. Creativity is the driving force of life.

And if you have to deal with repetitive situations, live them in a different way each day.

Change.

Change things. And if you cannot change things, change the way you do things.

And your essence will be reborn.

And like the phoenix that rises from the ashes, it will grow wings and finally fly.

And having an essence that flies is the most brilliant way of evolving.

JESUS

215

A Phase

Do not let this phase pass you by.

Do not wait for it to pass.

Do not think that all this discomfort and sadness is going to disappear with it.

Each of the phases of life we experience is to be enjoyed, felt, and integrated.

Integrate all these events into your energy.

Open your energetic structure to fit in all the things that happen to you so that they move you, so that they change you.

This is the best phase for your soul. It likes change. It likes to be reharmonized.

Allow this phase to change you, to reharmonize you.

It will show you the being you will become if you manage to feel and work alongside it. Do not spurn the power of this phase.

Do not opt out of the evolution it is offering.

And once it is over, once you have crossed those turbulent waters, sooner or later you will discover a new world, and you will realize I was right after all.

JESUS

216
Two Options

Picture a battle in far off times.

Imagine that you have five thousand soldiers.

Imagine that your enemy also has five thousand soldiers.

There are two things you can do:

Either attack, although having the same number of soldiers means the battle will be a bloody one and you are likely to suffer many casualties.

Or stay put—and although you may win yourself time, you run the risk of being attacked—aware that the strategy of defense does not have the same assertiveness as the strategy of attack.

How do you choose?

Both have advantages and disadvantages.

If you choose through the ego, any choice you make may backfire on you, resulting in unnecessary damage.

If you choose through the soul, despite the number of setbacks you suffer, these will always act as a guide in your evolutional path.

How to choose? What is ego and what is soul? How can you tell?

It is simple.

Place your consciousness inside your heart and remain there.

Feel one of these options. How does your heart feel?

Happy? Sad? Heavy?

Now do the opposite. Feel the other option, and notice how your heart feels.

I am certain that by doing this you will be able to reach your soul.

It talks to your heart.

And if you work toward bringing these two together, you can be sure you will evolve until the end of your days.

JESUS

217
Your Element

You did what had to be done. In spite of everything, in spite of the difficulties, the obstacles, and your own resistance, you did what had to be done.

In spite of the sadness.

Especially in spite of the sadness.

You did what had to be done to return to your original frequency, to return to your element, to return to you.

For a person who is not in his element is not centered, he does not focus on his energetic center and stops living humanely.

Because life is an adventure, but only for those who are able to focus inward. You may lean on others, and there are times when you may even move out of yourself, but you have to go back.

You have to know how to return. And, most important, you have to enjoy going back.

You have to like what you find, because if you do not like it, you will not want to stay there.

And those who do not want to stay run away.

They escape. To others. To things in matter. Do not forget that matter is similar to a film. It has light and color. It has sound and movement.

Inside you it is dark. There is neither movement nor color.

But it is subtle and bright. And subtlety and brightness are the keys to heaven.

Every time you focus your attention outward in pursuit of this film, in pursuit of life, you are going in search of movement, of light and sound, and you are descending to the frequency of matter—which, just like films, is pure illusion.

Up here is where truth lies. Within you is where truth lies.

Inside this seemingly dark and heavy dimension is the key to your happiness.

And the more time you spend there, the better you will understand it and the more you will value your brightness and subtlety.

You know that matter is anything but subtle.

And not long from now, when you have learned to respect your inner dimension, when you have learned to go back, you may begin to laugh again.

For now, stay there. Stay inside yourself. Choose yourself before everything else. Stay. Stay.

And one day, as a result of knowing yourself so well, of feeling so much, you will understand that there is absolutely no other place you could go.

Because I am there.

JESUS

218

Temple

Every moment you spend with yourself, your things, your thoughts, your questions and, eventually the answers within this book is a sacred moment.

You are a temple.

The whole of the molecular and energetic structure that makes up your being was designed to be a temple.

Where you pray. Where you recite. Where you meditate.

Where you internalize things. Where you are and where you respect this state of being. Where you cry and where you laugh, but above all where you believe.

Where you believe that everything will work out, that all endeavors carried out in the name of evolution will bear fruit and that one day you will be very happy.

You will be very happy because you have respected yourself, because you spent the time you were supposed to spend with yourself, driving away illusions and ghosts and facing the difficult reality of being who you are, with all the limitations and disenchantment this entails.

But also because you have admitted that inside this temple there lies an immeasurable amount of faith and truth and to live within these is to reach the realm of heaven.

Take care that the time you spend on your own is a great time.

Tend to each detail of your temple. Tend to what enters and what leaves.

Pay attention to what enters. Nourishment is very important and can change the constitution of your cells . . . and consequently your vibrational frequency . . . and moreover your energy.

The energy of those who surround you also determines your well-being.

Pay attention to what leaves. Do not move completely outside your temple. Do not leave it abandoned. Go out, go to others, but return. Always leave a path leading back. Never forget to leave the door open. So that you may return.

So that you can feel pleasure in returning.

So you can stop abandoning yourself as you have been doing throughout these last centuries.

JESUS

219

Energetic Plot

Everything you do to others is a result of their having attracted it to themselves.

Regardless of how little they want it, for it falls outside their comfort zone, no matter how hard you find it, because you feel sorry for them and end up feeling guilty, what you do—or are driven to do—is part of the cosmic game of attraction and repulsion that animates life.

Down there, there is a powerful energetic plot at work.

There is someone who needs a good shake. Needs to lose something. To reach rock bottom. To access the pain of the soul. To liberate the suffering that has transformed itself into energetic blockage—and this energetic blockage is easily identifiable because of the web that matter is made of.

This person needs a good shake so that this knot can be completely undone.

And you, on the other hand, have reached a point in your life where you feel a need to be by yourself. You will have to stop focusing so much on others. You will have to refocus on yourself. You have been outside yourself for far too long. You will have to say no to others so that you will finally be able to say yes to yourself.

Through the combination of both your energies, you and this other person come together, and you are led to say no.

You are led into leaving this person to his own devices. You are driven to rupture.

As you do not know that he needs to be given a good shake, you feel guilty. You think you could have done things differently to avoid him suffering. You believe you could have stayed there a little while longer. And you blame yourself for this.

But things are the way they are.

You do not do the things you do by chance. Do not think that your actions are disconnected from the Universe that surrounds you.

You are led into doing things. It is time to do what needs to be done. You need to act. And you feel that energy of rupture.

You perceive that it is time to change the course of events. And you act accordingly.

You risk loss. You risk guilt. But you take action.

And it is this act of yours that is celebrated by heaven.

Down there, you may actually think there was something else you could have done. But we up here know there wasn't.

Someone needs a good shake, and we chose you to do it.

Without guilt. Without fear.

And so you go on living and understanding that there is a time for things to happen and that time has now arrived.

JESUS

220
Going Slowly

I am here.

In truth, I am always here.

You just have to prepare yourself to receive me.

All you need to do is prepare to receive my energy.

Slowly.

And in order to slowly receive my energy you, too, have to be like this . . . slow.

So that your cells open up to receive me. So that on opening up, they release all the heaviness they possess. All the negativity.

And I will absorb this negativity, and I will switch the poles.

Where there was dark, there will now be light.

Where there was sound, there will now be silence.

A void.

And it is in this void that the soul will manifest itself. And I will be in this manifestation, in all my magnitude. In all my plenitude.

For it is in each cell that I exist as a whole, and it is the sum of those cells that makes me who I am.

Absolute energy.

And it is by being there in that place on earth and vibrating so high that you move closer to heaven and encounter me.

JESUS

221

Lessons

"I know that I have to go through this, but there was no need for that person to have done that to me."

Or . . .

"I know that I have to let go, but there was no need for that person to have acted like that."

Or . . .

"He didn't have to be so heartless."

Or . . .

"They didn't have to be so drastic."

". . . so fast."

". . . so unpleasant."

". . . so shameful."

". . . so sad."

I know that you would love to learn your life's lessons in a simple, pleasant, and colorful way, just as they appeared in your schoolbooks.

But it happens that life isn't like this.

You realize that you have to learn, you know that it is others who will teach you, but you continue to wish the lessons would be gentle. Peaceful.

I have something to tell you.

The Universe may actually be peaceful. It may even be gentle.

It does not have to be heartless, drastic, quick, unpleasant, shameful, or sad.

It would be none of those if you had learned your lessons the first time around.

The first time the Universe tries to show these things, it is soft and gentle.

But seldom do you understand. Matter is heavy and dense.

You are heavy and dense. Any sign that is soft is completely overlooked.

You receive the sign, and, as if it were no more than a gentle breeze, you continue to move swiftly and happily toward the precipice.

And so the Universe needs to speed things up. It has to raise the stakes. It has to lower the frequency. It has to become heavier.

It all depends on how much resistance you put up.

The harder you try to stay in a situation that does not give you back your original energy, the more the Universe strives to make you return home. To return to your path. To the place where your destiny and your creation undeniably lie.

So every time you believe that what you had to go through was too drastic, think about how upset the Universe is for having to be less subtle in order to teach you a lesson.

Think of how resistant you are and how hard it is for you to go back to vibrating in your energy.

And at the very least, think about how far you push me away from your life each time you refuse to learn the first time around.

And how sad I feel when this happens.

JESUS

222

Sadness

I know you are sad. I know the feeling won't go away.

I know things are not as you would like them to be.

You would like things to be easier. You would like them to be more helpful. You would like to experience them and be able to identify everything more clearly. Each feeling, each emotion.

Of course you would. But life, by way of a sacred movement that only life itself knows, that only life controls, is not giving you what you desire.

It is not letting you flow. It is not making things easy for you.

Life, for reasons that only life itself understands, does not allow things to work out the way you want them to.

And there is nothing you can do about it. You cannot change the natural order of things.

You can only feel sad. You can only feel regret. You can grieve, but that is all.

Nevertheless, you are capable of relating to your powerlessness and understanding that if there is something you are unable to do in your life, it is because it was all planned out this way.

It is life that is bringing you this powerlessness. And instead of focusing on what you are unable to achieve, look at the work you have to do in order to understand and accept what you really cannot do.

People and objects all have their own energy. They move forward in line with their own energy. And they cannot change their energy just so they can follow yours, just because you want them to. Just so you will not suffer.

Accept this. Cry, kick, scream, but accept it.

And instead of crying because things are not the way you want them to be, cry for not having the power to will them to be as you want.

And in doing so, you will be working on your powerlessness.

And you will grow.

And at least all that pain will have meant something.

JESUS

223

Mountain

Picture a man walking along a road.

The road has contours, bends, upward and downward slopes.

Now imagine that the man comes across an extremely difficult obstacle. Large. High. Wide. A mountain.

What does he do? He has three options.

Either he tries to pummel the mountain until it turns to dust.

Or he turns back and pursues another path.

Or he chooses the most difficult option of all: he climbs the mountain and goes over it without straying from his path.

In the first option, the man tires himself out, and if he actually succeeds in reducing the mountain, he will be so exhausted that he will lack the strength to continue on his journey. And the journey will end there.

In the second option, the man is frightened by the mountain and turns back. So he leaves his path.

In the third option, the man climbs the mountain. He has only one choice. To climb. But to climb it he needs to rid himself of his load. Free himself of things, let go of the elements he believed were essential for this journey. To climb, he has to accept that he must "be."

And he becomes lighter. The higher he climbs, the more load he sheds and the lighter he becomes. And when he finally reaches the top, he is truly liberated. From up there he may look down upon the whole horizon. And he understands that he is different. He cannot climb down to return to the path he started on. He must continue from this point onward.

And when he truly feels this, it is at this point that a new journey is opened to him. Tall, light, free.

When he accepted that he must climb the mountain, he was not aware that he was raising his energetic level.

It was only when he arrived at the top that he realized he no longer had to go back down. The journey would commence from this point.

Life is exactly the same. When an obstacle appears, you can avoid it by changing path but not vibration. Or you may face it and confront it with all your limitations.

And remember that to confront the obstacle with all your limitations does not mean to judge or criticize. It means you accept all your limitations and try to make each day a better day—but without overdoing things.

And it also means that you stop focusing on your limitations, so that you can discover your abilities, for where there are limitations there are also abilities. And when you have faced this obstacle and released density by accepting your limitations, you will raise your energetic frequency.

And your journey will never be the same again.

JESUS

224
Ascending

Ascend, ascend, ascend.

Come to me.

Ascend through the gateways. Each one will open in order for you to cross over, completely purifying your energy.

And upon passing each gateway, the more subtle your energy will become and the more you will feel me when you arrive up here.

Meditate. Ascend.

Leave your sadness down there. Leave all your worries, all your follies, all your pride, resistance, and ego down there.

Down there, leave all those things that limit you as a person, all the things that curb the truth and your soul's dignity.

Leave all that down there and come up here.

And on your arrival, I will have a great feast waiting for you, in honor of the conviction you have shown in ascending up here, and so that you may forget all the years you have spent down there without knowing the meaning of the word love. And after this climb, when you return to your life, you will be so different, so utterly transformed, that you will emanate a more peaceful energy. And this energy will go on to change the world. And everything will be different.

And you will realize why it is important to ascend. And you will recognize my touch, which transforms all things. You will feel it.

And never again will you look at your life and believe it is impossible to change things.

You will know that you have to ascend, that you should come up here whenever possible.

For you belong to a group of people who have been chosen to transform the world. To transform it through your own transformation.

And I am counting on you to carry out this task.

And I know you are ready for it.

JESUS

225

Stopping

You have to stop. I am telling you that you have to stop.

Stop running from the things that worry you and the things that hurt you.

Stop rationalizing in order to avoid feeling.

Stop transforming your days into dense and dramatic whirlwinds.

Stop. Stay. Alone.

Begin to acknowledge that it is important to stop. And that it is a priority.

Begin to acknowledge that it is essential for you to be like this, alone.

So that you may feel who you are. So that you may align yourself with your essence's highest vibration.

So that you may align yourself with your highest vibration.

For if you are aligned with your highest vibration, you will be able to access what heaven holds in utmost esteem for you.

And if you can really understand this, you will grow faster and go much higher. As you can see, to remain like this, still, quiet, within yourself, is one of the quickest ways to evolution.

And when you are there, at a standstill, motionless, and can really feel yourself and profoundly recognize your vibration, this will be the time when you are finally able to carry out the most beautiful projects in life.

And it is at this point that you will realize that you can be yourself.

And it is at this point that you will realize that it was worth stopping.

JESUS

226
Imagining

Let nothing enter.

That is the secret.

Let nothing enter.

Imagine a day when your energy is entirely resolved, completely focused, absolutely clear and emancipated.

Imagine a day when your energetic system vibrates through your unique and unmistakable frequency. It vibrates through "one," the energy of your soul, and remains unchanged like this, for better or for worse, immune from outside interferences, from different dispositions and from matter.

This is all I would like you to do.

Nothing else.

And as I know that it is in fact quite a lot, I am going to give you a tip.

Do not let anything enter. Try not to let in the information that you receive in matter.

Do problems crop up? Then send them back without allowing them to move into your energy. Sort them out without changing yourself, without allowing their dense energy to sully your own energy.

Is there some sort of conflict? Sort it out without allowing it in.

Look at it, knowing that it is of no real importance, it is what it is.

Do not allow it to disturb your life.

Make sure that this "not allowing it to enter" is for real, from the inside out, not just rationalizing your emotions.

Of course there may be times when you are unable to do this, when you are unable to stop things entering. Obviously, there may be some cases in which a conflict hits you hard and deep, but even then you will know what to do.

Cry, open your chest, and remove the density.

Do not blame anyone. If the energy of conflict has entered, it is because there was a memory of pain to let go of. And once this is done, go back to your center. Become focused. Go back to feeling your energy and try not to allow anything else to enter.

This is one of the biggest secrets in life.

And one day, when nothing—absolutely nothing else—enters to disturb you, when only love, affection, and sensitivity enter, at that point you will have finished your purpose on earth and you may come up to heaven without fear of being drawn back onto the wheel of incarnation.

And at that point, your spirit and your soul will reunite definitively—for the experience in matter will have ended—so that together they may continue their journey toward eternity.

JESUS

227
Reenergizing

Calm your mind. Relax. Just as you are now.

Stay like this, gradually feeling all your muscles. Feel each and every one of your cells moving slowly.

And you will slowly come into contact with all the things around you that vibrate ten centimeters from the ground.

Things and people that vibrate higher up.

You begin by connecting with the high energy around you.

You ask me what you should do in order to connect. You only have to feel. Feel your energy profoundly.

You need not think about anything. Just feel.

But do not allow yourself to feel dense, heavy, dark energy.

No.

Feel around you—with your eyes shut of course—for a higher energy. A purer energy.

I am sure you will be able to sense it.

And stay like that. Simply feeling it. Allow that higher energy inside you.

And then, once you are vibrating in this energy, look for people and things that have the same vibration.

Do not leave the place you are in. Do not open your eyes. Imagine the outside. It may be in the trees or in animals. Feel their vibration.

Feel it, and pull it toward you.

This is a recipe for reenergizing. Do it. Now.

And what does this message have to do with my question? you wonder.

Nothing at all. But this is what I wanted to say to you today.

JESUS

228
Signs

There are many people who believe that life works through signs.

If things go well, if they flow, you should go ahead with them.

If they do not flow, you should abandon them.

And there are many people who pay no attention to these signs.

But once they realize that coincidences do not exist, they attempt to "read into" life.

By way of signs, of course.

But that reading is still very rudimentary: "If everything works out, move forward. If there are obstacles, go back."

And they apply this formula to everything. And since they are open to life's signs, they think the ego is under control. This could not be further from the truth.

If life is easily "legible," why hold the Higher Self and the Essence in such high esteem?

Because only they can answer your most profound questions.

Whatever goes unanswered by your Higher Self and your Essence is answered by the ego, and therefore it will not be resolved.

So think along these lines:

There is something I must do, and that something requires a lot of commitment on my part. So life is going to come up with various obstacles in order to test how committed I am.

Imagine that during this time you give up because you feel that the obstacles are a sign for you to step back.

Do you see why it isn't so cut and dried?

And now you ask:

How can I tell when the obstacles are a trap to test my commitment and when they are a sign that things will not work out?

How do I know?

Your Higher Self. That is the answer. Only your Higher Self can tell you what to do. Only your Higher Self can point out the parameters of that initiative.

If you are still unable to connect with your Higher Self, use your intuition.

Never use your mental dimension. Never use your ego.

So now that I have explained the basics of coincidences and signs, let me kiss your forehead so that you may feel at peace.

JESUS

229
Counting on Us

It seems that you are trying too hard.

You are putting a lot of effort into things.

You put a lot of effort into everything.

May I ask you a question?

Why do you not count on heaven?

"Because heaven isn't going to give me what I want," you reply.

And I say to you, if you count on us, if you believe in us, then whenever heaven does not give you something, it is only because it was not meant for you.

JESUS

230
One Thing

Try to dedicate yourself to one thing only.

Do not worry about anything else.

Do not bother with anything else—other than your daily chores, of course. Focus on nothing else.

Do one thing and one thing only. And this one thing will go on to fill your meditations, your inspirations. Pay attention to all the details. Every one of them.

Place your love in all that you do. Place your love in this one thing that occupies all your thoughts.

And most important, show your gratitude.

Gratitude for being alive, for being able to profoundly live this experience.

And through gratitude, you will come to me.

And I will descend through that improbable channel you created with your gratitude.

And I will be there in an instant.

And I can personally help you to arrange this action, this event.

And whatever you do will have my energy.

And my energy will flow from you and your actions.

And everyone will feel my energy.

And you will finally become a channel for transmitting pure energy.

This is your mission.

JESUS

231
Discarding Your Dead Self

You have a "self" that is dead inside you.

Discard it.

Simply stop being who you were.

Dispose of your masks.

Thrust aside your insistence, your habits, and your obsessions.

Discard everything that is old, and you will realize it is dead.

It was already dead, yet it was inside you.

Look for something new to do, new adventures and new experiences.

Ask your Essence what it wants you to do.

Ask it what it feels.

Ask it what it wants to be.

Ask it everything, and then do what it tells you to do.

And it will take you to a path that is brilliant, even, and clear.

A path of light that just happens to be your original path.

At this point, your ancient self will no longer exist.

You will feel new things and vibrate at a much higher frequency.

And things will begin to happen within your cells.

And things will begin to happen in your life.

Everything will be in its place.

All this because you agreed to discard your dead self and were willing to go in pursuit of your eternal self, which was always there although you could not see it, could not feel it, and thus thought it had gone away.

But it had not and never will. This is your self that has always been here but is now purer, clearer, and more together.

It is the one you should follow if you truly wish to start your journey toward heaven.

JESUS

232
Thank You

Thank you for all your blessings.

Thank you for this incarnation.

Thank you for being able to vibrate in matter.

For learning from it.

Thank you for the vibration.

Thank you for the incredible emotion, good or bad, strong or weak, which I am allowed to experience every day.

Thank you for the days.

Thank you for the pain, which, once freed, transforms into joy.

Thank you for the night, which, once lived, transforms into day.

Let everything be exactly

As it is meant to be

So that I may arrive precisely

Where I can see

The Light

Where I may have

Light.

JESUS

233

A Pact

Let go of the "self" that controls. Let it go. Give up controlling events. Give up trying to control everything.

No matter what it is, whatever it is that you are trying to control, let it go. Entrust.

Entrust yourself to me so that you may feel safer. There are people who are unable to hand their pain over to heaven. It is too abstract. If you feel this way, entrust yourself to me.

But really entrust yourself. Let go of everything.

Have you noticed that the harder you try to control a situation, the further it slips from your fingers? These are the opposites—the duality of matter working at its best.

Let go of the "self" that controls. Let it go. Give it up.

Learn to flow with life, to allow things to flow. And once you have understood that control will take you to where you should not go, you will understand that it will never lead you to the place you should go.

And that is sad. It is very sad because if you do not let go, you will inevitably return there, life after life after life, to find your stride and discover your own frequency, which will bring you up here to your place in heaven.

Let it go. Entrust yourself to me. Turn yourself over to heaven. Make yourself readily available to energy. To light.

Free yourself from violence and from resistance. Let all of this go forever.

And this is a pact you make with yourself.

A pact with energy.

And a pact with the light.

JESUS

234
Rising

Listen to the bells tolling.

Do you hear them?

They are approaching to announce that you are ready for the next journey.

For the next plane.

For the next level.

No, you are not going to die. You are simply going to rise to another level in this life. To another frequency.

All your cells are vibrating faster as a result of the experiences you have had and the purification you have been through because of them.

The energetic world is ready to make you rise, up high to the level of vibrational frequency.

And up there, it may actually prove to be harder for you, given that you continue to live down there in everyday matter.

But that is the challenge: having exemplary energetic behavior.

Do not adjust things so that you can be more comfortable.

Face your fears. Do not try to control events.

Do not control people. Do not manipulate.

Do not do anything you cannot be proud of.

This is my advice, the advice of an ancient wise man whose aim is for you to live in a healthy, spiritual way, down there.

Above all, find your essence.

Make it a priority in your life.

Talk to it and listen to what it wants.

And once you begin to realize that it makes you happy, move ahead. Do not be afraid.

It may be one of those rare occasions on which you are given the opportunity to get to know your soul.

JESUS

235

The Call

Life is calling you.

Life is calling you to move out of stagnation.

Life is callling you to new and great adventures.

All you have to do is say yes. You need only agree to make a commitment to honor what you came to earth to do, which is to be who you truly are. As long as you can be who you are on every occasion, the rest will fall into place.

Come and see life.

Leave that cocoon, that vast but artificial feeling of comfort that you have entered into.

"If I do not take risks, I will never lose," you think.

And neither will you ever gain, I say.

So close your eyes, breathe deeply, spread your wings, and learn once and for all that learning how to fly begins inside you.

JESUS

236

Agreeing to Receive

Agreeing to receive. This is the issue. You are all used to giving, and that is where control lies. When you are giving, you are controlling how events evolve. You are controlling events and you are controlling the people you are giving to.

"While he is receiving, he is accepting me. He is not rejecting me," you say.

By limiting yourself to giving, by trying to control other people's affections, you begin to block.

Those who believe that only giving is important become blocked.

They become blocked because they do not let go of control.

They do not relax or receive.

To receive is to lose control. To receive is to accept. It is to be aware that there may come another time when you need to, yet no longer receive.

It is to accept that you may end up at someone's mercy. You may feel vulnerable, and you may suffer.

And you do not want to suffer, do you?

I understand, but think about the fact that you are not receiving anything to avoid that suffering.

And if you are doing all this to be accepted, to avoid rejection, you need to realize that by not receiving you are actually attracting rejection.

Think:

How is it possible for someone to end up attracting rejection when he has gone to extremes to avoid it?

Think.

My advice:

Open up. Open up to life. Stop controlling. Allow yourself to receive.

People want to give to you. But you are closed. You prefer not to receive so as not to lose control. You prefer to be needy and in pain.

People want to give, and you are suffering. This can't be right.

Open up.

Open up.

Even if it hurts you, open up.

Even if you become needy, open up.

Even if you feel bad, open up.

Even if you believe people will hurt you, open up.

Even if they hurt you, open up.

Open up. This is the only reason you are there.

This is the only reason you have not yet raised your vibration to be closer to me.

Open up.

Always.

JESUS

237
Reprogramming

So that you may have new experiences.

So that you may experience new situations, new emotions—and you know that new emotions are the only thing that will make you change, that will radically change your life.

New emotions will reprogram your brain.

Which will reprogram your cells.

Which will reprogram your organs.

Which will reprogram your body.

Which will reprogram your life.

Which will reprogram the lives of those close to you.

Which will reprogram your town.

Which will reprogram what the world is like energetically.

Which will reprogram the Universe.

And everything that exists has but one objective, and that is to reprogram the Universe.

Note: Read the message that follows.

JESUS

238

New Emotions

So that you may experience new things, experience new situations, and new emotions.

Read the previous message and then return to this message.

It is no use trying to look for new energetic incentives in life.

All the things you can have or do in your present life can change the way you feel, but only for a short time.

An event happens outside you; it provokes an emotion within you. You go through this new emotional experience, your energetic system perceives that change is on its way, it feels insecure and begins to demand your old energy back, and you quickly return to your old ways.

Your belief system, which activates your defense system, is so powerful that rarely does someone permanently elevate his vibrational frequency on account of something that comes from outside.

It is very difficult for this to happen.

But the opposite couldn't be fairer—but it is also more difficult. It goes like this:

First you reach a new synthesis, a new way of looking at things.

Then you believe in this new synthesis. You begin to incorporate it into your energetic system and your thought process.

You begin to vibrate at this frequency.

And you reprogram the Universe.

JESUS

239

You

This is what you are going to do today: You are going to put on some music you really like.

You are going to sit in your special place, a place in the house you feel is yours. A place that allows you to be who you are and where you do not have to make allowances. A place that makes no demands on you and allows you to be.

Simply to be.

Sit in that place, close your eyes, and call upon yourself.

You are going to summon your true self. Do not think about it. Do not make it up. Just feel it.

Summon the energy of who you are. The person you truly are.

And watch. Observe. Feel. Above all, feel.

Who is this person?

Do you recognize yourself?

Is this person you? Or do you still need to go further to be that person?

What are the things this person thinks about?

Are they the same things you think about?

And how does this person think about them?

Is it the same way you think about them?

And what does this person feel?

Can you feel what this person feels?

Is this how you feel?

What does this person believe in? And what about you?

Does this person believe in me?

Does this person love me?

And what about you?

Let this person come to me.

Let this person rise.

And now, you rise, too.

JESUS

240

Feeling the Love

We are going to meditate. Come. Come and meditate with me.

Sit somewhere cozy. Where you feel very comfortable.

Put on some music you enjoy.

Close your eyes and breathe in deeply a few times.

You do not need to visualize anything at this stage. Instead, feel a light invading you. A pure light, a healing light.

When you feel light and cleansed, begin to think about all the good things you have or have had in your life.

The emotions and fantastic experiences that you have allowed yourself to have throughout life.

The best days.

The best nights.

Summon the energy of the people you have loved and continue to love in this life.

Even those who were not always good to you but whom you loved.

Even those who hurt you but whom you continued to love.

Summon the energy of all those people. And feel the love.

Feel the love you have for them.

Acknowledge that regardless of what has happened between you, they are here in your life to teach you how to love.

And to honor the love that is inside you.

They are in your life to show you that you have all that love inside you to draw on.

So that you may love without expecting anything in return.

Rather than being something you use to barter, love is a blessing for those who feel it. For those who can feel it. Simply feel it.

Hold on to the energy of those people. And love.

That is all. Love, love, love.

And regardless of their response to your love, you will feel your energy changing vibration and ascending.

And when your chest is on the brink of bursting open because of all the love it emanates, raise your conscious and come show me your love.

For you can love me only if you love others—love their souls—and are able to love life.

Therefore, when your chest is almost bursting with the love you feel toward humanity, regardless of all its many flaws, you will immediately be loving me.

And loving yourself, for you are part of that immensely imperfect yet magical race called humanity.

JESUS

241
Realization

You may not realize it, but the situation you are going through is following a pattern.

It has a vibrational frequency. It has an energetic tone.

You need to understand this.

Regardless of who got you into this situation or whether you got yourself into it.

Regardless of whether someone hurt you or you hurt someone.

Regardless of whether someone made you suffer or you caused the suffering of others.

Regardless of all this, you have to realize that this situation is not unique in your life and that the emotion it triggers in you is not unfamiliar.

You may not have experienced this specific situation in this lifetime, but you have almost certainly gone through other situations that have the same emotional load.

What you are feeling right now, regardless of by whom, when, and how it was provoked, regardless of the existence of any external issue to do with the heart, that thing you are feeling right now is something already familiar to you.

More than familiar, it is something that is yours.

It is an emotion from your soul, a density that has not yet been resolved, and now and again it comes to the surface so that you may understand that it remains unsolved.

Therefore, stop focusing your attention outside yourself.

Get hold of that emotion that is so familiar to you.

Forget other people. Stop thinking about things and circumstances.

Focus on your chest. Focus and pull on that emotion. Pull. Pull. Feel. Feel.

And when that feeling takes over you because you have decided to accept it as yours, it belongs to you. Then and only then will it be time to remove it. To get rid of it.

Realize this:

You will never be able to get rid of something that you do not accept as your own.

This is a concept you should carry with you throughout your life.

First accept that it is yours. Then remove it.

"And how can I remove it?" you ask.

And I reply, "Relinquish this emotion. Regard it as yours, but not from this lifetime. It is from bygone times and is no longer of use here."

Relinquish it. Realize that you no longer need this emotion in order to be the person you are. That emotion is not creative, it is not positive. And today, your heart has room only for positive, constructive emotions that help your soul move toward evolution.

Relinquish what you are feeling.

Stop thinking that others have put you into this situation.

Realize that it is you who puts yourself into this position every time you cast others as the villain.

Understand this, and you will become closer to the truth.

JESUS

242

The Weight of the World

Do you know why your back hurts?

Because that is where you carry the weight of the world.

The weight of all those people you want to save—and believe you can save.

The weight of all the things you wish were different without understanding that they are this way because your energy asked them to be this way, so as to trigger things in you that you must work on.

The weight of your insistence that all those around you be fine—without understanding that it will make no difference if they are not.

All this has a name. The weight you carry on your back has a name.

Guilt.

Guilt is when you try to take responsibility for other people's choices and for the type of life that those choices attract.

You can take responsibility for only two things, the choices you make and your life. And nothing else.

All the rest is simply a way of escaping from the responsibility you have in your own life.

It is easier to look at others or, more to the point, at the mistakes others have made. You look outward in order to avoid looking inward.

Because it hurts inside.

And that is why your back hurts.

On the day you allow yourself to look within in a direct, mature, and responsible way, that will be the day you can stop focusing on what is outside yourself, stop making demands, and cleanse your guilt. And who knows, maybe in the place where your back hurts, there will appear two wings that were restrained and now have permission to help you fly.

And on that day I will be waiting for you up here to show you heaven.

JESUS

243
Discomfort

It is in the midst of great discomfort that you will find your greatest skill.

It is in that dreadful place of total discomfort that you will discover tolerance, patience, and accessibility.

When you choose to accept discomfort, you also choose to be tolerant. You choose to be patient. You know that it is going to last—even if for a short time—and you agree to go through it.

And learn. And cleanse. And live. And experience.

And after you have lived through the drama, after blood has been spilled, you will know that you have survived, and from here on, your relationship with fear will be forever changed.

JESUS

244

Choosing for Yourself

Have you ever noticed the power a choice has? When a person chooses in favor of himself, based on who he is and because he wishes to validate himself?

When a person chooses for himself, for the light he has, there is no outcome that can shake him.

No obstacle can make him feel unmotivated. And since this choice comes from within, from the depths of his essence, it has an overwhelming force.

And it creates self-esteem. It creates self-love, self-construction.

It creates energy for making more and more choices.

When the energy of choice liberates itself, it creates a wave of movement in the direction of the Universe.

A Universe that gives back a calm and pacifying energy in abundance.

And others are blinded by his light. And heaven is enriched with each day that passes.

This is the power of choice.

The power of helping the Universe to grow.

JESUS

245

Calling Me

Your communications are so conscious . . .

This means that you have reached the levels that are needed to touch me.

For me to touch your heart, your energy.

For me to replace the centuries of cellular patterns of dark energy you have.

For me to present you with resources for purification.

You have changed your tone. You have changed your resonance. You have raised your vibration.

And today, when you so effortlessly arrive up here, do not think it is your imagination. I am here to explain what I have come to do.

Feel my answer.

Listen to my version.

For life's events have more than one purpose.

Everything is intertwined and perfect so that you will be inspired to eliminate everything that is not a part of you.

Call me, and I will come. I will make your days more colorful.

Fill them with meaning. I will come and instruct you on the best way to live in matter. I will come and bring you a love that is pure and bright and within your heart, the information you need at this point in your life.

Call me, and I will come and fill you with my light and make you shine like the stars.

So that you do not forget where you have come from. So that you do not forget who you chose to be.

JESUS

246

The One Way

In reality, there is only one way of doing things.

There isn't a variety of ways so that each of you chooses your own. The different ways you act simply reveal how diverse the human race is.

There are no two ways of doing things, for the opposites define the duality in matter.

There is only one way of doing things.

And all the others are merely the paths which you take to get there.

They are formats from down there, dense, lacking the high frequency that is required of aspiring spiritual beings.

There is only one way. And that is to feel, feel, feel.

The more open your sense of feeling is, the better.

The more you respect this feeling, the better.

The more you realize this is your true self, the self that chains cannot hold down and that concepts cannot sway, the better.

The more you celebrate this extreme sensitivity, the better.

There are no two ways of doing things.

There is only one.

And that one way has everything to do with me.

JESUS

247

Movement

When everything is wrong, focus on yourself.

When everything around you is falling apart, recall how the movement of the Universe makes things around you fall apart when it wants you to search yourself.

It is an endless movement. You move outside your energy to find safety in others.

Everything that is outside you is easier.

Everything that is outside you is comfortable.

It is safe.

It is much harder to focus on yourself. For inside you there are sadness, sorrow, resentment, and admonishment. Inside, there is darkness. Inside, it is cold.

So it is understandable that you flee from within as fast as you possibly can and grab on to others.

However, by attaching yourself to others, you are provoking a reaction in the Universe.

The Universe cannot allow you to remain outside yourself.

Therefore, it will have to remove the feeling of security that you are used to feeling in your relationships with others.

And how does the Universe remove this sense of security?

It is simple. It shatters your illusion that these relationships are highly satisfactory.

And how does the Universe shatter this illusion?

By disappointing you.

Suddenly, for no apparent reason, people you trusted so much get angry at you, they ruin things, they do not pay you enough attention, they become sick, they die.

This whole movement of losing people or, more to the point, the illusion of having an idyllic relationship with others, serves only one purpose.

To make you look within yourself. To feel your own energy.

It makes you see yourself. It makes you create someone you would like to be. That you would be proud to be.

Indisputably, all this movement places you in your own emotional dimension.

It makes you feel.

And through feeling, regardless of whether it is pain or joy, you will be forced to open up your channel.

This feeling will force you to rise through this channel.

It will teach you to come up here and obtain safety in heaven, the only place that can really provide you with a sense of security.

Among the beings of light.

In your Higher Self.

And ultimately in me.

JESUS

248
Loving Me

Love me.

Life's enchantment resides in the love you feel for me.

And the love you feel for me brings you closer to my energy.

And you rise higher.

And you rise purer.

Love me.

Feel only this love for me.

And you will see how this love will break down personal barriers, destroy castles, walls, blockages, and discrepancies.

It will rip off binds and restrictive archetypes.

Love me.

Feel. Choose to feel that immense love for me, without desiring anything in return, not even the light of my presence.

For even a desire for me to love you or show you my love is something that resides outside you.

Just love me.

And allow this love to invade your life, your body, and your energy.

Allow this love to invade other people and the earth.

Allow this love to grow and invade heaven.

And when you least expect it, when you believe that it will go no farther than this, you will receive a surprise.

I will descend through the channel of love you have emanated.

And on a calm night, I will come and lie by your side and whisper stories from up here, from heaven, in your ear.

And your life will change from that night onward.

And you will never need to be alone again because you have touched the essence of life and gained your own light, which will forever keep solitude at a distance.

JESUS

249

Crying So You May Stop Losing

What does it mean to cry?

To cry is to remove the negative energy that, being inside you, led you to attract the particular situation that has left you feeling sad.

And by removing this energy—based on the principle that you always attract the same energy you emanate—you will stop emanating it and you will therefore stop attracting it.

Recognize the cycle.

For example, you have energy inside you, violent energy. You will emanate this violent energy. As a consequence, you will attract the same or a corresponding energy. In this case, you will attract violence.

You have two options:

You can get angry with the person who hurt you, focusing your attention on someone outside yourself and not on reaching inside or cleansing, thus continuing to emanate this energy.

And so, following the natural order of events, you will continue to attract this because you continue to emanate it.

Or you can realize that this situation has left you feeling sad— you do not judge the person who has hurt you—and you allow yourself to cry over this sadness, removing the energy from your chest, and by doing so, you stop emanating it.

And so, following the natural order of events, you will no longer continue to attract violence because you have stopped emanating it.

As you can see, crying is the basic principle. The rest simply falls into line.

Looking at the example used:

You receive violence.

You cry because you have received violence.

You remove the violence from your chest.

You stop emanating it.

You stop attracting it.

It is simple, isn't it? But difficult to carry out, I know.

That is why human beings were born with an ego. When the ego understands and makes a commitment to the light, it has enough power to do what I have suggested . . . and much more.

So you may start right away.

Cry.

It will do you good.

And I am up here just in case you need anything.

JESUS

250

Being Reborn

You are being reborn.

In all senses, in all forms, in the most trivial of day-to-day activities, you are being born again to a new life.

You are gradually coming closer to me.

You are gradually becoming more evolved, purer, and more subtle. You are gradually reaching the dimension of the sky where fairies can fly.

This is the time of rebirth. It is the time for men to understand their mission.

To recognize that man's true mission, the only mission possible for human beings within humanity, is to be capable of being unique, distinct, and sacred.

It is to be able to stand out from the seven billion other people on earth.

Be authentic.

Be organic.

Be special.

JESUS

251

The Day of Essence

Today is Essence Day.

It is the day for you to play with your essence, to give it your undivided attention and to take it seriously.

On an evolutionary level, your Higher Self is the master.

He is the one who can teach you. He is the one who has your life plan up in heaven, the plan you should turn to when in doubt.

But when it comes to self-esteem, earthly experience, and self-realization, your essence is the grand dame.

It is she who knows what will make you happy down on earth, with the resources you have been given there.

It is she who has your life plan for your earthly life and is responsible for your executing it as creatively as possible, creating a new self every day, or, at the very least, rejuvenating it each and every day.

And today is her day. Do something you have wanted to do for a long time.

Be courageous. Have the audacity to go after what makes you happy.

Go. Do it. And offer your boldness to your essence. Offer it to her.

Show her how much you like and trust her.

Talk to her. Ask her what she wants you to wear today, how she would like you to wear your hair, and so forth.

You will see how that little white ball inside your chest begins to speak. To tell you what it wants and why it is here.

Take a day to be with her. Put her ahead of everything else in your life. And you will see how you will begin to fortify one of your greatest allies in heaven in its everlasting task of making you happy.

JESUS

252

Your Love for Me

Your love for me will save you.

The love you feel for me, the light that comes out of your heart, is what is best in you.

And by loving me you are bringing out the best in you.

Hence, the more you love me, the more you vibrate in that extremely high frequency that is love and the longer you will vibrate higher up, bringing out what's best in you at a cellular level.

And we already know that the more a human being gives of himself, the more abundance he receives from the Universe.

So by loving me, you will be receiving that love from the Universe.

And that love saves.

JESUS

253

Raising Your Vibration

Basic emotions have a very low vibrational frequency.

For example, when you are enraged you vibrate incredibly low—and where there is a low vibration, there is a lot of density.

When you are attached to something, for example, your vibration is extremely low.

Density is very high. When you raise your vibration, you detach yourself from people and objects and entrust everything.

"What has to be will be. It will be what is best for everyone. Whatever will be, will be."

At this point, you raise your vibration. You let go of violence.

You vibrate higher. You shine brighter. And you become much closer to heaven.

JESUS

254

Loving Me, Loving Yourself

Love me inside you. For I am inside you. I am there in every part of you, in each and every cell.

And it is only when you reach deep into yourself that you come into profound contact with me.

And it is only when you love yourself eternally that you are able to love me eternally.

For when you lost me two thousand years ago, when I disappeared from your life, you no longer thought yourself worthy of anything—since you were not worthy of me. That was your reasoning, which has lasted until now.

But that was not my intention. I moved out of your lives in the hope that my absence would force you to look inside yourselves and understand that I was there.

And on realizing that I was inside you, you would love me and come to love yourself, since you now realized that you were indeed worthy of my presence inside your energy.

And today the choice is still yours. Either you continue to miss me externally, focusing on my absence and consequently believing you are not worthy of my presence in your life.

Or you understand that you do not see me so that you may feel me inside of you and love yourself because of this.

There is a choice to be made.

And only you can make it, no one else.

I can only clarify things for you. I cannot choose on your behalf.

I have made my choice, and that is to love you eternally, no matter what you choose.

And I will always be here.

Waiting for you.
Waiting for you to understand.
Waiting for you to choose to love me and to love yourself.
Waiting for you to surrender to the light.
Waiting for you to feel that I am the light.

                                                      JESUS

255

Expectations

Remove all expectations. From everything. From everyone. Stop expecting things to be a certain way.

Stop expecting people to be a certain way.

Stop inventing things in your head or creating illusions.

This only serves to activate your control, your manipulation, and your ego.

Imagine you stop having expectations about life. From this moment, you will feel that everything life gives you is a blessing, since you expect nothing in return. And so you will be able to feel grateful for all that life gives you.

Because you do not feel that life is obliged to give you things.

Imagine that you stop having expectations of people.

If they fail you, you remain calm, for you expected nothing from them.

If they are kind, sincere, and loving, if they show themselves to be friends, allies, and accomplices, given that you were expecting nothing, you would be able to see and thank them for these acts.

Human beings have too many expectations and feel that what they receive is never enough. They would like more. They believe they should have more.

And that desire for more ruins everything. It makes people calculating, competitive, and petty.

And in this state, a person feels only resentment. He is not grateful for anything and does not receive anything because he already believes that things are his to start off with.

And this person will receive more disappointment than joy. He will feel greater resentment than gratitude.

And a soul without gratitude is absolutely stagnant.

JESUS

256

Before Waking

A lot of things happen during sleep.

Your soul does not communicate with your brain. Instead, it speaks to your heart.

The communication it has with your heart is direct and clear, free from intermediaries or manipulation.

Communication between the heart and soul flows, for the heart understands the soul and, more important, it feels it. And the soul loves to be felt. It loves to be understood and taken seriously.

Your soul carries your life plan there on earth. Your mission.

It is entirely aware of what you still have to accomplish and whether you have strayed from your path—or are still on track.

Clearly, communication with the soul is crucial for those who wish to begin or continue on the evolutionary route.

However, your mind and your ego are not interested in doing this. Your ego is a force of survival and, as such, is interested only in the immediate and in being comfortable. Its task is to make you feel good and keep you away from pain.

However, the problem is how it goes about doing this. More often than not, it tries to carry out its mission in an immediate and, I believe, cowardly fashion.

It forces you to run away.

It makes you run away from pain, even when it is bursting from your chest and there is clearly no escaping it.

It makes you run away from emotions, and we know that those who run from emotions end up becoming blocked and sick.

It makes you run away from confrontation, turning you into a hypocrite and liar.

It makes you run away from the unknown, making you self-indulgent and lazy.

It makes you run away from sensitivity, making you cold and hard.

It makes you run away from spirituality, making you lose yourself and your sense of direction.

In short, it makes you run away from your soul, making you sad and soulless.

And what has all this to do with sleep? Everything.

It is during sleep that the ego is least switched on and the soul has a chance to manifest itself. It is during sleep that important secrets about the way our soul feels, how we really feel in regard to things, people, what happens to us, and the state of our lives are revealed.

It is during sleep, whether we dream or not, that what is most profound in us has the opportunity to reveal its reason for being.

So from today on, before you are completely awake, when you are still feeling drowsy, in that moment when you cannot quite open your eyes because they feel heavy, in that moment, instead of jumping out of bed for another supersonic day, stop.

Stop and be still.

Keep your eyes closed for two minutes, just feeling things.

Just receiving what the night has brought you. It does not matter if you do not remember the dream you had. For the first few minutes after you have woken up, stay with that sensation—an emotion, a frequency within your chest.

Stay. Feel it. Recognize that this is a communication from your soul. It is what it wishes to say to you today.

If you feel tightness, a strange sensation, fear, or discomfort, do not run from it. Do not activate your ego, your mind, in order to flee from this ever-so-subtle communication.

Stay. Feel. Cry if you feel the need to.

Imagine that you are opening your chest and removing the density, the darkness, the heaviness inside. Respect what you are feeling. And now you are ready to start your day. You may go about your life with the certainty that you have done something for your soul, that you have taken a step in the right direction toward your own evolution, which will inevitably bring you closer to happiness.

JESUS

257

My Thanks to You

I would like to thank you for all you have done for the earth by raising your vibrational energy.

I would like to thank you for all you do for the earth each time you choose yourself, choose the light. Every time you step away from the things that are not part of you and do not vibrate in you, it acts like an inner magnetic field, significantly raising the energy of the earth.

I would like to thank you for the time you put aside to work on yourself, consulting my messages and really making the effort to understand this new logic.

I am thankful for your faith, your availability, and your dedication. For going to where it hurts and believing that it will quickly pass.

Thank you for the emotion.

JESUS

258
Misconceptions

Things are not always how you want them to be. Others do not always see things in the same way you do, nor do they put the energy you desire into things.

Formally speaking, a person may have the same opinion as you on a subject.

I say formally, because it has a form.

Only a form, nothing more.

This person may agree with you formally, but the energy he allocates to the issue may be completely different from yours. This is what I call a misconception. You believe someone did something with a specific intention, when he not only intended something altogether different but believes you do things with the intention he has in mind.

Complicated? Not really.

Do this:

Regardless of the formal agreements you have made with people, regardless of whether you agree on almost every point—and I say almost because no one is ever in total agreement, am I right? Regardless of all this, feel the energy.

Close your eyes, allow me to enter and feel. Feel the other person's energy. Feel your energy. Feel each of your energies in relation to the issue at hand.

And I promise you that a great synthesis will emerge from this meditation.

Now you know what to do.

Now you may move forward.

JESUS

259

A Hole in Your Heart

I realize that when people are in love, they wish to experience the profound emotion that comes from two people sharing.

They have a desire to experience the incredible sensation of being alive, of their chests bursting open with emotion, of seeing beauty in flowers, of feeling that life is inconsequential and love is all that matters.

But that is not how things work.

Human beings have a need mechanism that functions in the following way:

They have a hole in their heart. A hole provoked by centuries of deprivation.

A hole provoked by karmic memory, life after life in which emotions went uncleansed and now call out to be cared for. A hole provoked by the absence of your Higher Self, your soul—which at the time of your birth remains up there in heaven, waiting for you to connect so it may enter and fill your heart.

A hole that is also provoked by the obliteration of the essence after so many centuries of looking outward, crying out to others, "Like me, like me . . ."

Well, this heart is now dark and cold. It is desolate and sick. And it is in pain. And the more it hurts, the less you go there and the less you relate to it.

Well then, what happens when someone falls in love?

Does the heart open up and explode with love from one hour to the next? No. Does a being tap into the love that lives in his heart regardless of the pain? No.

He simply feels ecstatic because he has finally found someone who sparks an emotion so strong in him that it is capable of filling the void he has.

This is not love. This is need.

The heart does not yet love.

The heart wants only to stop hurting.

And since this is not love, it cannot last long. And even if it does happen to last, it is unlikely to be very fulfilling.

Once the heart realizes that this person who is supposedly loved does not fill the void, it will begin to make demands, discussions will arise, and confusion will settle in.

Remember this:

No one can fill the void in another person's heart.

No one can receive love if he emanates need.

First you have to restore your essence. You have to go deep inside your heart, work on your karmic memories—from other lives—which provoke pain.

Only then will true love show itself.

And at this point, I guarantee that a beautiful event will take place.

You will experience the greatest emotion of your life.

The greatest emotion of your lives.

JESUS

260

A Toast to You

Look at how energy moves when the things that are meant for you begin to approach.

Look at how things change shape. Clearly, you have changed your energy. You have spent a long time trying to correct yourself, trying to harmonize yourself, and, most important, trying to break patterns.

To break patterns. That is the key.

Patterns as old as time, insistent on manifesting themselves in this lifetime.

And these patterns follow you everywhere.

They manifest themselves in your behavior and attitude.

Patterns that make you function on automatic pilot, never questioning yourself, never knowing why you do things, never feeling.

You have spent a long time breaking those patterns in your life.

You have accepted transformation.

And now I would like to make a toast to you.

I am going to celebrate the fact that you have succeeded.

You have turned things around and moved closer to the light.

Needless to say, there is still quite a way to go until you get there.

But I am going to let you in on a secret. As long as you are down there, there will always be quite a way to go until you get here.

But what matters is that you have already started your journey, and that will carry you to the other side of eternity.

Now, at this moment, observe how energy moves in your favor.

Receive heaven's blessings.

Receive what I have to give you.

Do not run away.

When energy arrives, do not think that it arrives by chance. Do not think that it is not meant for you, that it is a mistake.

Accept that it is me. Accept that I sent you this in gratitude for the times you focus on yourself.

Receive the blessing.

And you will understand how much good you have done humanity by accepting to elevate yourself just a little bit higher.

JESUS

261
Time to Receive

Enjoy what I send you.

Not everything needs working on.

Not everything is suffering. Trust that when the lesson is well learned, great blessings will soon arrive. What I am sending you this time around may be very colorful. It may be good. It may make your soul smile again if you know how to take advantage of it, if you stop making judgments, thinking that you do not deserve this, that it is not meant for you.

"I want only what is meant for me. What the Universe has to give me," I sometimes hear you say. Even if you do not hear yourself, I hear you.

Well, this is for you. I sent it to you. You attracted it with your new energy.

You worked, reached deep within, and transformed yourself.

Now is the time for this blessing. It is time to receive.

And when you are ready to take advantage of this, when you are enjoying it, remember that throughout every bit of this experience, there is a touch of heaven.

JESUS

262

Discovering Sadness

When someone is very angry at you, when he thinks you should have done something in a certain way, be aware of this:

That person is in pain. His heart hurts, and since he has no experience in dealing with the heart, he ends up feeling extremely angry. "I can control this rage," he thinks.

But rage destroys your central system, which deprograms and then needs to be fed more rage.

It is a never-ending cycle.

And the pain remains unexplored and is not cleansed or cried over.

Grief is set aside.

Would you like to help?

When someone is very angry at you, ask that person: "Why are you sad?"

And help him give way to this pain. To his sadness. And as he begins to yield to the pain, he will begin to let go of his rage, for it was there only to protect him from giving way to his pain—regardless of all the consequences rage attracts. As this being yields to his pain, he will begin to let go of violence. And naturally he will stop attracting violence.

Would you really like to help?

Do as follows:

When someone is upset with you, find out why, help that person yield to his sadness, and give him a hug.

And stay there, comforting him throughout his pain.

And neither of you will ever forget this day. And your souls will remain friends forever.

JESUS

263

Getting in Touch with Yourself

Get in touch with yourself.

Although there is still a lot that needs to come out, your energy is much more refined now.

If you wish, you may now get in touch with yourself. Your original energy can make itself felt. It can show itself, and let me tell you that at present there are very few people in your situation who are able to do this.

Most of them are so full of karmic waste that they do not stand a chance of catching even a glimmer of their original energy.

Get in touch with yourself.

And the more you practice this exercise of getting in touch with yourself, the more you will activate your original energy and the more complete you will be in your own things, your life.

I know it is hard to focus on oneself when you have spent the last centuries focusing on others. But you have come a long way to get to this point. And now finding yourself is the last leg of your journey.

And I am here for whatever you need, absolutely anything you need.

JESUS

264

Two Major Lessons

I can understand your need to act on what you are feeling.

To allow life to flow, to accept a change in direction. To let yourself flow in the direction the wind takes you, guided by the movement of life's magnetism.

I understand and accept.

I accept and give my blessing.

However, you have to realize that although I tell you that you are entitled to this—and, in fact, that I teach you to fight for this right—I need to warn you that life is not going to be easy.

Those around you want assurances.

They are as you were in the beginning.

They want emotional assurances. They want security.

They are more attached to you than to themselves.

Thus they do not want you to change. Your change will tear down their certainties, shake up their lives.

They do not like chaos. They do not know that you truly change only when you accept chaos, when you accept that you no longer need to be the same person today that you were yesterday, and that you have to reinvent yourself each and every day. Only by accepting this can you move toward evolution.

Others have plans for you.

Plans that will not disrupt their lives too much. And your changing is definitely not part of their plans.

What should you do?

Change, pursue your path, and upset all those around you or leave everything as it is and risk dying of boredom, consumed by monotony, with an essence that is both coarse and dull?

Remember this: there are many times in life—many indeed—when saying yes to others may mean saying no to yourself.

And you came to earth to evolve your own soul, not those of others.

I know that you do not want others to suffer. I understand this.

But consider that they, too, have to learn. And if they do not do learn through you, they will have to learn through life's lessons, and these lessons can be taught through your own actions.

Confused? Let me explain.

Imagine that we up here perceive that it is time for person X or Y to detach. It is time to promote emotional detachment so that this person will finally take notice of his essence.

This person needs to attract emotional loss in order to detach.

And imagine that you are also learning to let things flow. To allow things to flow is to listen to yourself, to give your essence priority. The scene is set: this person needs to detach, and you need to let yourself loose in order to discover yourself.

Naturally, you will be that person's loss. The more you feel a need to leave, to no longer depend on anyone, to allow life to flow in another direction, the more that person will feel he is losing you and begin to feel desperate.

In short, with only two events—your life flowing and you learning to respect yourself—I promote two major lessons:

Fruition and internalization for one person and detachment and internalization for another. Have you noticed how internalization is always present?

So when you believe that the need for your own life to flow better causes others to suffer, consider that this may be how it is meant to be. It may actually be heaven's intention.

And that the action that you take may be about someone else's evolution, and we up here have a name for this energetic entwinement: fate.

JESUS

265

Coming Home

It is time to come home.

To return to your garden, your old aromas, and your old flavors.

It is time to leave the adventures on the outside, tie up the horses, and withdraw the infantry.

Come home.

Return to the warmth of the fireplace, to the comfort of a heated house. The soul needs a little warmth right now.

The soul needs to reenergize, to gain strength to face and overcome the new challenges that lie ahead.

Come home now.

For the moment, the task has been completed. It is time to rest.

Put away your weapons.

And return home to your warm bed, so that your essence may rest.

For it is by resting that a warrior reestablishes himself and receives new visions of entire universes that have yet to be discovered.

JESUS

266

Not Wanting

Do not want to eternalize life.

Enjoy it.

Enjoy every moment that life has to offer you.

Every minute is magically sealed by me to give you everything your energy needs to develop.

With each moment you wish would last forever, you are denying the new experiences being presented to you.

Do not wish to perpetuate things. Just enjoy each moment.

And show gratitude. Be grateful for being alive so that you may enjoy your incarnation.

That is all.

The rest will come of its own accord to make your life more colorful.

JESUS

267

Judging

To judge is to believe people could be different from the way they are.

It is to believe they could be diverse, more acceptable to you.

It is to want people to meet your expectations so that you can avoid stepping out of your comfort zone.

To judge is to believe heaven made a mistake when it placed that allegedly unpleasant person before you.

It is to deny you may have attracted this person. It is to refuse the possibility that you may have attracted him in order to gain a greater understanding of the energy you are emanating. And it is a refusal to accept that it is you who needs to change in order to stop attracting this.

To judge is to deny the perfection of heaven, energy, and the vastness of time and space.

To judge is to believe your tiny ego knows everything, including what should be happening. And as a result, you renounce what is happening.

Clearly, to judge is one of the biggest evolutionary counter-movements.

So why do you insist on judging?

JESUS

268

Music

Put on some music you enjoy listening to.

Elevate your soul to me, and come and dance.

Come and meet me up here in this magical context of light, and let your essence fly.

Allow it to express itself in the vastness of heaven.

And because of the love you feel for this music, I am going to find your heart up here, and I will have the chance to save it from sadness, from coldness, from melancholy, and from violence. And when your heart returns to earth, it will be filled with me, and the sadness will have disappeared.

And you will be able to see each thing for what it truly is, now that you no longer have this burdensome filter, which casts a shadow over everything you see.

And you will be able to feel clarity.

And my image, my energy, and my love for those who, like you, are not afraid to come to heaven for inspiration will be forged forever in your heart.

JESUS

269

Losing Your Expectations

Have you noticed how the harder you try to avoid creating expectations about things—the harder you try to behave well and allow life to flow—the more your ego tries to match this?

You may try not to create preconceived ideas about things. You may even consider—and accept—that you have no hold on the future. Even so, your ego—your internal controller—has only come to a standstill. It is motionless but not inactive.

To be inactive would signify that it would stay as it is. It simply remains like this, without doing anything. Like this, still, waiting for life to present itself.

But it is not still. It has stopped moving, yet it is waiting for something to happen.

And this something has to be very strong for it to be so motionless.

Well, this continues to be your ego trying to gain control.

You renounce knowledge of what the future holds—with the benevolent attitude of someone who is giving up something that is within his reach—but the future is not within your reach. So how can you renounce something that is not within your reach?

But this is what your controller is like. It makes great attempts to deliver something that does not belong to it.

You forsake knowing what will happen in the future, yet you remain in anticipation that something will happen, and you still wish to control the relevance of this event.

Let me tell you something:

With that attitude, nothing is ever going to happen. Nothing at all.

There is no use waiting.

There is no use controlling.

And let me tell you this, you will not reach the kingdom of heaven with that kind of attitude.

JESUS

270

The End—and a New Beginning

It is the end.

The end of great hopes and great illusions.

It has to come to an end. Allow the things that do not move, that do not evolve, to come to an end.

Whatever fails to evolve naturally does so because it is not meant for you. And if it is not meant for you, let it go. Let it go.

Let it go.

There are things that are yours and want to manifest themselves. They are rapidly approaching and want to reveal themselves. They want to show themselves. They want you to accept them into your life without apprehension, without hesitation.

Yet from up here, they see you full of certainty, full of resistance, and beset with a great fear of change and of all things new.

And you do not let go of the old because you cannot see anything new approaching.

And the new does not move toward you because you do not let go of the old.

Do you see the irony in this?

If you continue as you are, you will continue the same small and meaningless life you have been living.

If you let go of the old and familiar chains, you will be set free into the air and carried to unforeseen places.

Where you will find what is meant for you. Where you will find what is yours. And what is yours is much greater than what your tiny mind can ever imagine.

Of that I can assure you.

JESUS

271
A New Beginning

A new beginning is opening.

A new beginning is opening to usher in a new spring.

A new perspective free from chains and old affairs.

A new reality is flourishing like the first few days of spring.

It is the time of spiritual spring, a time when all things are born, when everything is budding and developing. A time when everything comes together in a way that is long-lasting and unprogrammed . . .

and uncompromised . . .

and unburdened . . .

but permanent.

A time when the resources needed to meet the stated objectives are scarce.

A time of choices. A time of reflection.

A time to begin the journey. The new journey that will take you to infinity.

Where the path is vulnerable but enlightened.

Where your step is uncertain but happy.

Where time is time and what you do with it will always count in your favor.

A new beginning is opening. Do not try to determine what it is.

Feel it.

Do not try to control life.

Feel it.

Do not wish to get to the end. Do not be hasty.

Feel it.

Walking this path is the only assurance you will have on this turbulent road.

JESUS

272
Flying

Fly toward the brightness, beyond the stars, beyond the constellations—beyond what the mind can imagine.

Fly beyond what your body can endure.

Accept detachment, accept the need to let go.

Fly beyond the brightness, past the portal of light.

Come to me.

Confer your heart on me. Confer your ability to love on me. Confer your strength on me.

Return home, and I will transform you into an angel. I will transform you into a being of light. I will transform you into an avatar.

And when you return to earth, things will never be the same again because you have filled the earth with heaven.

You have filled the earth with me.

JESUS

QUESTION ARCHIVE

Here you may record the questions you asked and the messages you received from *The Book of Light*. Do not forget to always include the date, your question, and the messages received. This is the only way you will see how things develop.

Date__/__/__Subject matter_____

_____

Date__/__/__Subject matter_____

_____

Date__/__/__Subject matter_____

_____

Date__/__/__Subject matter_____

_____

Date__/__/__Subject matter_____

_____

Date__/__/__Subject matter_____

_____

Date__/__/__Subject matter_____

_____

Date__/__/__Subject matter_____

_____

Date__/__/__Subject matter_____

_____

Date__/__/__Subject matter_____
_____

Date__/__/__Subject matter_____
_____

Date__/__/__Subject matter_____
_____

Date__/__/__Subject matter_____
_____

Date__/__/__Subject matter_____
_____

Date__/__/__Subject matter_____
_____

Date__/__/__Subject matter_____
_____

Date__/__/__Subject matter_____
_____

Date__/__/__Subject matter_____
_____

Date__/__/__Subject matter_____
_____

Date__/__/__Subject matter_____
_____

Date__/__/__Subject matter_____
_____

LIST OF MESSAGES BY TOPIC

READERS CAN CONTACT ALEXANDRA SOLNADO TO RECEIVE MESSAGES OF LIGHT:

Subscribe to our site www.alexandrasolnado.net and receive messages that Jesus dictated to accompany you on your spiritual evolution.

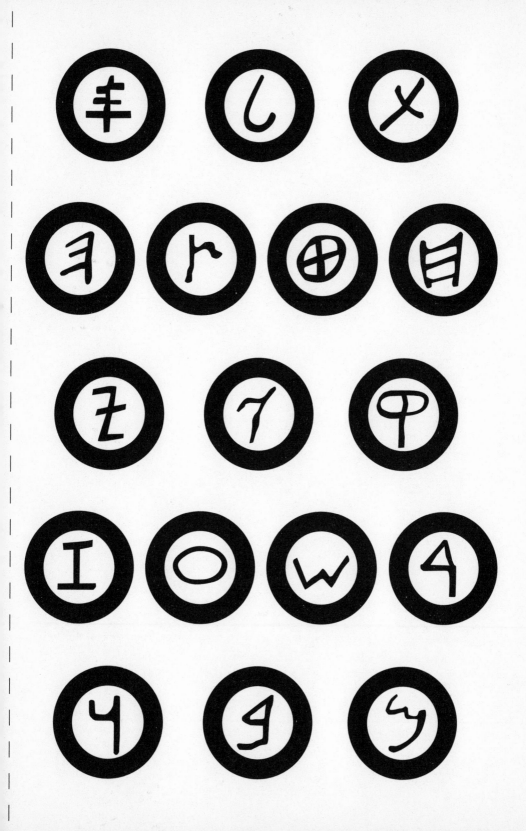